MOREEN Shoff

FABULOUS

Books by

John Lee Weldon

FABULOUS

THUNDER IN THE HEART

THE NAKED HEART

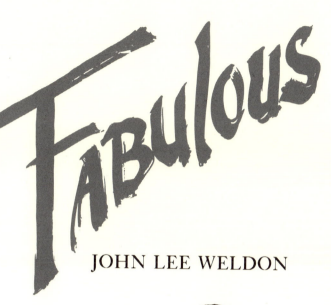

JOHN LEE WELDON

PAUL S. ERIKSSON, INC.

New York

*For all pet lovers
and especially bird lovers*

TABLE OF CONTENTS

FABULOUS

I BUY A HARLEQUIN

In mid-flight he gave me a certain look. I felt something tugging inside me. He was irresistible. I had to have him.

Was there a chemical attraction between us? Interpreters of love sometimes attribute that wondrous feeling to body-chemistry. Can a feeling of real love exist between a bird and a man?

Yes. And this is how it happened:

He was in a large flight-cage with fifteen or twenty other parakeets. They were a lively and colorful batch of blues, greens, yellows—fluttering, feathered rainbows. This one, the one who caught my eye, was mostly white. His wings were white with black markings. His tail feathers were white, tipped with deep blue and black. Light blue feathers covered his belly, and when his wings were open, I could see the same shade of light blue feathers on his back. The feathers on his chest, neck and head were white. There were little black ridges of feathers across his forehead, indicating that he was a very young bird. His eyes were two black lights, sparkling, full of life, two tiny bubbles of glittering charm. The cere was a very light blue. He seemed to be a bit smaller than the others.

The owner of the pet shop was standing next to me.

"That's the one I want," I said, pointing.

"The harlequin? He's a beauty," she said.

"Harlequin?"

"That's what they are called when they have sort of splashes of black on white. Like a harlequin. There are other types, but this is one of the most beautiful . . . honest to God, it is one of the most beautiful I've ever had in my shop."

"Last week I saw one in the cage in the window. It was all white except for two small blue dots on each side of its chest."

"That's what is called an albino. Not a pure albino. Pure albinos are solid white and have pink eyes. Whites that are not pure albinos have reddish eyes. Sold the one you mentioned the day after I put it in the window."

"I thought about buying it."

"You'll be just as pleased with the one you've chosen."

"How old is he?"

"All of these you see in the cage are between four and six weeks old."

This was Wednesday, April 10; I set his birthday as being March 1. It would be an easy date to remember.

"Young, healthy birds like these are the best to choose from," she said. "They're easier to train."

She was a round, warm woman and pleasant to deal with. She carefully opened the door of the large cage and put her hand and forearm inside. But the bird I had chosen was not to be easily taken from his companions, perhaps some of them were his brothers and sisters. Her hand almost closed over his wings, then he darted away from her. There was a scurrying and fluttering and squawking-chirps from all the birds. However, after three of four efforts, her hand managed to close around his body and wings, and she brought him out of the cage. Quickly she placed him in a small cardboard box with airholes in it. For a minute or two he fluttered and scratched his feet on the cardboard. Then he was as quiet as a mouse.

"Have you ever owned a bird before?" she asked.

"No."

"Then you'll need a cage and all the supplies. Take your choice. The bird is $3.95. The cages run a little more. I'll get together some of the things you'll need while you decide on a cage."

I chose a square white cage in the shape of a house; the roof sloped on each side and was removable. There were four wooden perches inside, and from the top center of the cage, there hung a plastic swing. The price of the cage was $4.98.

"Since you've never owned a bird before, I'd like to give you a few helpful hints about taking care of him," the owner of the pet shop said. "Sometimes I've refused to sell a bird to a customer, afraid he'd frighten it to death, let it starve, or give it to some brat to maul. But I have a feeling you are going to be good to the bird."

"I certainly hope to be. But how much time and attention does it require? I work in an office for a living and I write in my spare time, so I don't have too much time to give it."

"The parakeet requires as much time and attention as you care to give it, and as little time and attention as you care to give, so long as you give it fresh food and water every day, and keep its cage clean."

"How often does the cage have to be cleaned?"

"You'll see. A damp sponge, not wet, just damp, will be good enough to dab away spots now and then. Once a month take the bird out of the cage. You'll probably be letting him fly around the room by that time, anyway. About once a month wash the cage thoroughly with soap and water. I use Ivory. Be sure it's dry before you let the bird back in the cage. Never wash the perches, scrape them clean with this perch scraper, it's only 19¢. I've put it here with his other things."

"Why shouldn't the perches be washed?"

"If the bird sits on a damp perch for a while, he may get a cold, or pneumonia, or arthritis. A bird can have just about any kind of illness a human being can have."

I was a bit frightened. Was I making a mistake in buying a bird? Frankly, I had never even thought about a bird being sick. Of course they die, every living creature is bound to die, but I had never seen a sick bird.

The lady must have noticed consternation on my face. "But don't worry," she said. "There are remedies; if he should get sick, let me know at once. Put a drop a day of vitamins in his water; that helps to keep a cage bird healthy. Here it is, here. And in this box is his regular food. You don't have to give him a full bird-cup everyday. Fill the cup the first day, then the following days

just brush away the shells from the seed with
your finger. Parakeets shell their seeds. Then
pour in a little more food. Once a week empty the
cup and wash it out and fill it up again. Here's a
tiny treat cup. Once a day give him his treat food,
this is it here, it's richer than his regular food, so
that's why the cup is smaller. Here's a cuttlebone,
he'll peck at that. It's good for his beak and bones.
Here's gravel paper, bird gravel and charcoal.
They are good for the bird's digestive system.
Now pick out a toy for him."

"A toy? For a bird?" I was surprised. Toys
were for children. I had seen dogs play with rubber bones, balls and old shoes; I had seen cats play
with strings and balls. It had never occured to me
that a bird would want to play with a toy.

"Certainly," the lady said. "You don't want
him to get bored, do you? This row of toys here
along the wall are all for parakeets."

I blinked my eyes. How in heaven's name do
you choose a toy for a parakeet? "You choose one
for me," I said.

"No. You'll like it better if you choose it for
him. You don't have to hurry about that though.
Think it over a day or two. Then come back and
buy what you want for him. He has enough to
keep his attention occupied for a while. He'll be
exploring his new cage and keeping an eye on
you."

"On me?" I was like an innocent child, buying
a toy for myself, not knowing quite what to do
with it, except to look at it and admire its beauty.

"Yes. You can make a real pet out of him if you

want to. Take it slow and easy. In time, he'll hop
upon your finger, crawl around your shoulders,
light on your head, and greet you when you come
in from work. I'll bet you live alone, don't you?"

"Yes."

"He'll be good company for you. Here's a little
booklet, it's free, it'll help you to learn how to
take care of him and train him. Oh, by the way,
what are you going to call him?"

"A bird. A parakeet."

She laughed. "A bird, a parakeet; some people
call him budgerigar or budgie. I mean, what are
you going to name him?"

"Oh, I don't know. I've never thought about
naming a bird." I had written several books and
given hundreds of characters various names, but
this was a new one on me. He was in the dark box
now, but I thought of his exquisite beauty. He
was really fabulous. I meditated for a moment
while she was putting the articles in the cage and
wrapping the cage.

"He's fabulous," I said.

"What? O, yes, he's a fabulous bird."

"That's what I'll name him. Fabulous."

When I arrived home I washed the cage and
sprayed it with No Mite Spray, dried it
thoroughly, and very carefully placed the perches where I thought they would please the bird.
I put the gravel paper and gravel in the bottom
of the cage, and filled his cups with food and
water.

I felt sorry for the bird being shut up in that

little dark box, but now I was ready to show him his new home. I placed the box on the door of the cage and opened the end of the box. The bird hopped out onto a perch in his cage, looked around in wide-eyed curiosity, then scurried over to the far side, placed one foot on the wire of the cage, leaving the other foot on the perch; he looked at me with a mixture of fear and curiosity. He was so frightened his entire chest and belly were visibly, rhythmically beating with fear. I spoke to him softly and told him not to be afraid, but he turned his head away from me. I made soft kissing sounds; he glanced at me, then turned his head away again.

I carried the cage into my living room and placed it on an end table next to my lounge chair. I picked up a book and leaning back in the chair, I tried to read, but I could not concentrate on the book. My mind was on the bird. He stayed in that spot on the far side of the cage. For nearly two hours I sat beside him, occasionally trying to read, now and then making soothing, kissing sounds at him, hoping he would come to the near side of the cage and let me know he knew I was his friend. I suppose I was expecting too much too soon.

I went into my kitchen and ate dinner, hoping if I left him alone for a while he would go to his food cup and eat. After dinner I returned to my chair beside him and looked at his food cup. There was no indication that he had eaten even one seed. He was still in that same spot on the far side of his cage. His heart and belly were still pounding.

I glanced at my watch, it was eight-thirty. The pet shop did not close until nine. I called the pet shop and told the lady that my bird would not eat and that his heart was pounding so much it looked as if it would burst right out of his body.

"I'm glad you called," she said. "It lets me know you are concerned about the bird, but don't worry about him. He'll eat when he gets hungry enough, and he'll stop being afraid when he realizes he's got a good home. Just leave him alone for a while, let him get used to his cage. He's probably trying to figure you out."

"All right. I'll go to bed early. If I stay up late, I'll keep looking at him. I have to work tomorrow and I am going to the opera tomorrow night. Will that be enough time away from him for him to get used to his cage?"

"It may be. Sometimes takes two or three days. There's a whole new environment for him to grow accustomed to, but a young pet will grow accustomed to a new environment quicker than a human being."

This was something to think about. I had never considered a bird or an animal to be more capable, in any way, than a human being. In time, this bird Fabulous would open new areas of thought for me.

I glanced at the bird again; I saw no sign of change. I took my shower earlier than usual; when I turned off the shower and opened the glass door of the shower enclosure, while reaching for a towel, I thought I heard a soft chirp, but I was not sure. Quickly I dried myself, and wrapping the towel around my waist, I went into the living room. If he had chirped, he had not moved. I picked up my book, turned out the light, and regretfully left the frightened bird alone. I went to bed and tried to read for a while before going to sleep.

The first thing I did the following morning was to take a look at the bird. I was glad to see that he had moved. He was on the same perch, but both feet were on the perch. When he first saw me he again placed one foot upon the far side of the cage, but after a second or two he took his foot down. I looked at his food cup. There were a few shells on top of his food. He had not eaten much, but at least he had eaten something. I could see the beating of his heart in his chest, but his whole chest and belly were no longer pounding. He was still afraid, but not nearly as afraid as he had been last evening. I felt a wave of relief.

I went into the kitchen to make my morning coffee. I filled the pot with water, and as I turned off the water—did I?—yes, this time I was sure I heard a chirp. He was coming to life, a sound of real life; nature's life was being heard in a lonely apartment.

That evening after work I had dinner in a restaurant near the old Metropolitan Opera House. After dinner there was time to kill before the doors opened at seven-thirty. I did a little window shopping. I was bored with waiting. My mind was on the bird. What was he doing? Was he eating, was he drinking? Was he taking a nap? Was he still frightened? When would he learn to like me? Maybe I should have bought a dog, a dog will usually take to you immediately.

I enjoy opera, but that night I was bored. The opera was "Boris Godunov"; I do not know if I was bored because of that particular opera, or because my mind was concentrated upon that new life in my home.

The opera was long and it was nearly one o'clock before I arrived home. I had left a light on in my living room, so the bird would not be in the dark before I put on his cage cover, or in the semi-darkness during the day if the sun became shadowed with clouds. Anxiously I walked down my foyer to my living room. He was still perched in his chosen spot. He gave me a glance, but only a glance. He put his foot on the wire of his cage, turning his head away from me. Then he put his foot down and gave me another brief glance. He was still afraid of me, or maybe now, he was not so much afraid as unsure of me. I examined his food cup. The top of his food was covered with seed-shells and there were a few on the bottom of his cage. He had eaten heartily. I examined his water cup and it seemed as if he had drunk a few drops of water. Gently, I placed his cage cover around his cage and went to bed feeling more relaxed. He would adjust.

The following day after work I stopped by the pet shop.

"So how's the bird?" the lady asked.

"I think he's going to be all right. He's eating well."

"I'm sure he'll be all right."

"I want to buy a toy for him. He won't pay much attention to me, maybe he'll pay attention to a toy."

"Give him time. Give him time. Which toy do you want?"

"That ladder with the bell at the top. Will he climb the ladder?"

"Of course he will."

"What about the bell? Why does it have a bell on it?"

"He'll learn to ring the bell. Just give it a tap, show him what it is, and when he's ready, he'll ring it."

As soon as I came home I put the ladder in his cage, bracing the ladder in an upright position against one of his perches. I gave the bell a light tap. He glanced at it but he did not go near it.

After dinner I again sat down and relaxed in my lounge chair; it is one of those chairs in which you may lean back in a reclining position. I tried to concentrate on a book, but my mind was on the bird. The bird was ignoring me and he was ignoring the toy I had bought for him. I was determined to make friends with that little bird. Could I have a snob living with me in my own apartment? I lifted the bird's cage and sat it down on my lower belly. At first, changing the position of his cage frightened him. But after a moment he seemed to relax. The cage moved up and down slightly with my breathing. He hopped down from an upper perch to a lower perch near his water cup and took a drink of water. This was the first time I had seen him drink. After he swallowed the water his head bobbed up and down. I laughed. My laughter caused the cage to bob up and down. He looked at me, not with just a glance, but a glint of what appeared to be amusement came into his eyes as he looked at me and heard my laughter. He took another drink, bobbed his head up and down, and looked at me again to hear my laughter again. Thereafter, anytime the bird heard me laugh an amused and pleased expression came into his eyes.

I suppose it was that evening when I began to fall in love with Fabulous.

Fabulous—an ounce and a half of beauty (the average weight of a parakeet), a tiny creature who became uppermost in my life, he was one of nature's exquisite works of art.

All that evening I sat quietly with the bird in his cage on my lower belly, with one hand placed on the side of his cage. Every now and then he would glance at me, and his glances were no longer so brief. Thus he began to grow accustomed to me. We began to grow accustomed to each other.

CHAPTER TWO

HE TAKES WING

The next morning I was having my usual cup of coffee in bed, when all of a sudden, from out of the quietness of the early morning, I heard a bell ringing. It was not the blazing ring of the door-bell, nor was it the blasting ring of the telephone. It was a lovely ring, it was music to my ears. I jumped out of bed and dashed into the living room. Fabulous was perched next to his bell-ladder, with one foot resting on the side of the bell. He looked up at me inquiringly; there was an expression in his eyes, on his face, in the position of his body, which seemed to ask: "Is it all right? May I ring the bell?" I was smiling and I made soft kissing sounds to him and spoke in a tender tone of voice, "Yes, ring the bell. Ring the bell again."

He rang the bell again, hesitantly, softly, pushing the bell with that tiny foot, gazing at me, not just glancing, not just looking at me, but gazing as if to see my reaction. I laughed joyously. He rang the bell a little more rapidly and his eyes were glittering like two black diamonds.

That same bell-ladder became one of his favorite toys, perhaps his very favorite toy, throughout his life.

Before going to work I reached my hand in his cage and removed his food cup to brush the shells away and give him fresh food. As I turned away I saw him hop down to the spot where the food cup had been and look at that empty spot; his head moved from side to side. As I was leaving the room, I saw him hop upon the wires of the near side of his cage, and I'll swear, he glared at me. When I came back into the living room with the fresh food, he was still on those wires of his cage. I placed the food back in his cage; he hopped down to a perch and watched me. He reacted in the same manner when I removed his water cup, took it into the kitchen and brought back fresh water. For several days his expression and action of consternation took place each time I removed his cups. Then he seemed to learn my purpose in removing the cups and was no longer worried. He knew I would return the cups with fresh food and water.

That evening when I came home from work, I again sat his cage in my lap and rested my hands on the side of his cage while I watched the early evening news report on television. At seven-thirty I went into the kitchen and ate dinner. After dinner I had a shower and returned to my lounge chair beside the bird. I was not content with his being beside me. I wanted him closer to me. Again I sat the bird's cage in my lap; this time I opened the door of his cage—he did not attempt to come out; I believe he already considered that cage as being his home, really his. I placed my forefinger on the same perch on which he was sitting, but two or three inches away from him. He did not hop off the perch, but he again cuddled against the far side of his cage and put one foot on the wires of the cage. He gazed at that finger for two or three minutes. Then slowly, hesitantly, he set his foot down on the perch. Slowly, hesitantly, I moved my finger a little closer to him. He put his foot back upon the wires

of his cage, keeping an eye on my finger, so I let
my finger remain still. He put his foot back on
the perch, not daring to take his eye off the finger.
With the utmost of care I moved my finger closer
to the bird. My finger was less than two inches
from him, when—oh-oh—that was enough. His
foot grasped the wires of his cage. My finger
halted. His foot came back down. For a minute or
two I did not move my finger. Then again I let
my finger slide closer, hoping, since my forefinger
is about the size of the perch, he would think it
was a perch. But he knew darn well that finger
was not a wooden perch. He permitted it to come
within a quarter of an inch of him. Then with
both feet he hopped upon the side of his cage and
glared down at the finger, and he looked at me as
if to say: "You've gone far enough. Now shove
off." For a minute or two I did not move my
finger. But he gave me another one of those
"shove off" looks, so I slowly let my finger slide
back and out of his cage. He hopped back down
on the perch and touched it with his beak, as if
to say, "This is my territory."

The following evening my finger invaded his
territory and received the same results. But with
my third attempt I achieved success. That evening as my finger moved closer and closer to him,
he kept a watchful eye on it, occasionally throwing me a brief glance, but his foot did not go upon
the side of his cage. When my finger was within
a quarter of an inch of him, he leaned his head
down and pecked it. I let my finger remain still,
pressed against the perch. He gazed down at the

finger as if to ask himself: "Is this going to be all
right or is it not going to be all right?" Then he
leaned his head down again and barely touched
my finger with his beak. It was not a peck; it
seemed to be a touch of examination. Slowly I
moved my finger over and touched his foot. This
was the first time I had ever touched him. He may
not have been thrilled by our first touch, but I
was. Lightly I pressed against his foot. He lifted
his foot and placed it upon my finger. I held my
breath and slowly moved my finger over to his
other foot. He stepped upon my finger. I heaved
a soft sigh of relief. Fabulous was perched upon
my forefinger, the finger, which in time, he came
to consider as being his finger, another one of his
perches, something that belonged to him as much
as it belonged to me.

Usually I write on weekends, holidays, vaca-
tions, or any other time I can manage to take off
from office work. However, I had just finished
writing a book a few weeks before I bought Fabulous, and I was not yet ready to start another
manuscript. Therefore, I could devote my whole
weekend to Fabulous. That Saturday morning I
sat for a long time with my hand in his cage, my
finger on his perch, while he sat upon the finger;
occasionally he would reach down and touch it
lightly with his beak, examining and re-examin-
ing that finger-perch, growing use to it, accepting
it.

Although the door of his cage had been opened
a number of times, he had never yet ventured to

come out. In the afternoon, I carried his cage into my bedroom which is smaller than my living room, also, my living room did not have a door on it. I closed the bedroom door and opened the door of the bird's cage. I stepped away from his cage, expecting him to dash out and take a flight. He simply looked at the open door and did not even come near it. I stepped a few feet farther away from him and made soft kissing sounds. He looked up at me and looked at the open door, took a few steps toward the door and peeped out, but he did not even stick his head out the door. Apparently, he felt more secure in his home-cage, but I wanted him to feel secure in the apartment; I wanted him to feel it as his home, too. For a few moments I continued my efforts at coaxing him out. He would simply look at me and look at the open door. And that was it.

Discouraged, I picked up a book, sat on the bed, and leaning back against the wall, I read for about an hour, now and then making those kissing sounds, hoping to lure him out. But obviously he had no intentions of coming out through that door. Then I remembered that the lady in the pet shop had told me the top of the cage could be removed by unscrewing the screws at the four corners of the cage. This I did, and stepped away from him.

He looked up. There was no top over him. There was space, space! His feet scurried up the wires at the front of his cage, and he perched on the top wire, looking up and around. He lifted his wings and he was up and off in a flight around the room.

Being born in an aviary, this was probably the first time he had taken such a long flight. But he bumped himself against a wall and fell down to the floor; my heart went up in my throat. (Later I learned that this is not unusual. I heard of a bird that had killed itself the first time it was let out of its cage by flying swiftly into a mirror.) Fabulous was dazed slightly, or perhaps more surprised than dazed. He shook himself, something like a dog shaking off water. Then he walked around the room, examining the floor, pecking at the cracks between the boards. I thought it best to train him not to play on the floor. He was such a tiny thing there would be a danger of stepping on him. I knelt down and reached out my forefinger toward him. He would have nothing to do with it, he was much too busy examining the grains in the wood of the floorboards. I crawled closer to him. He spread his wings and flew upon the bed, looked up, and took a flight around the room; again he bumped himself against the wall and fell to the floor. (However, that was the last time he ever bumped himself against any wall. He learned.) Fluffing his feathers and shaking himself out of another daze, he again seemed to be fascinated by the cracks between the floorboards. I tried again to get him to hop upon my finger, but he was not interested. I was determined not to let him get into the habit of playing on the floor, so this time I put his cage down in front of him, about two feet away. He took a look at it.

His own private home. Rapidly his feet ran over to his cage, up the front wires to the top wire, then down the wires inside. He glanced around the inside of his cage. Yes, everything was all right. He hopped down to a lower perch and took a drink of water, bobbing his head up and down. The lights in his eyes were dancing. His heart was beating fast, not from fear, but with excitement and the exertion of his first flights around the room.

Now he preened himself.

It was a joy to watch him preen those beautiful feathers, cleaning them, getting them in order, dolling them up. Between his beak, his tongue touching the feather, he would take a long wing feather by the root and slowly slide his beak and tongue to the tip end of the feather. Sometime later, I many times watched him take the root of a long tail feather between his beak; his beak sliding down the tail feather, the feather curved around, then when he reached the tip end of the feather, he let it go and watched it pop back straight. Then he would take the other side of that same feather and repeat the action. He seemed to enjoy watching it pop back in place; I know I did. I would have thought it a tremendous job for him to clean all those feathers, if I had not, through observing him, realized how much pleasure and pride he took in preening himself. I felt sure Fabulous knew he was beautiful.

Sunday I let him out of his cage again. I opened the door of his cage, but, no, he would not come out the door. He watched me while I unscrewed

the top of his cage. As soon as I lifted the top
away, up the wires his little feet ran, and when
he reached the top wire he paused only for a split
second, then he took two or three flights around
the room. This time he did not bump himself and
he did not fall on the floor. He landed on top of
a wrought iron bookshelf. His feet (which are
primarily toes) curled snugly around the
wrought iron. His beak reached down and
touched it, examining it. That wrought iron
bookshelf was soon to become one of his favorite
landing places. He learned to enjoy climbing
along the wrought iron and from one shelf to
another. I let him stay out for about two hours.
He was excited and thrilled—the tone of his
chirps, the expression on his face and body let me
know this. He would take a flight around the
room whenever he wanted to, sometimes he
would land on the foot of the bed, then again he
would land on the top of the bookshelf. He would
walk sideways along a shelf, looking at the books
as though he wondered what they were, now and
then giving one a peck. His beak was quite an
examiner. It was becoming beautifully clear that
the parakeet has an immense curiosity.

When I was ready for Fabulous to go back into
his cage, all I needed to do was to hold the cage
close to him, and in he would go.

Fabulous soon got over his objections to going
in or out the door. The door was a flip-down type
and he often perched on it as though he were a
young gentleman sitting on a porch.

CHAPTER THREE

GETTING ADJUSTED

I had bought a bird instead of a dog or a cat because I did not think I had much time to spend with a pet. I thought a bird would be merely something to look at and listen to its chirping, a bit of life in the apartment, life other than myself. However, I found more and more time to spend with Fabulous. Every evening when I came in from work, the first thing I would do was to let Fabulous out of his cage.

During our third weekend together, I spent most of my time with Fabulous. While we were in the bedroom, after one of his long circular flights, he lit on the wrought iron bookshelf, on the shelf second from the bottom. He cocked his head around at me and gave me such a sweet, beguiling look, I got down on my hands and knees, on a level with him, and slowly crawled over and lightly kissed him on his left wing. He made no objections. So I held out my little finger to him, holding my four fingers in a position slanting upward. He looked at the fingers, then looked up at me; his eyes seemed to be asking, "What do you want me to do?" I let my little finger touch one of his toes; he put one foot upon the finger; I slid my finger toward his other foot, then he stepped upon my finger. Gently I pressed the next finger against his stomach; he looked at it, then hesitantly placed a foot on it, then another foot. I let him get his footing secure before I placed another finger against his breast. He looked at the finger, then looked up at me, questioning, wondering what to do. "Come on up," I told him in a playful tone of voice. He stepped upon a third finger. Then I pressed my forefinger against him. Hesitantly, he put one foot on the finger, then took it down. "Come on up," I encouraged him. He hopped upon the forefinger. He was at the top of the finger-ladder. He realized, he sensed, his instinct told him, that he had accomplished something. He had learned to finger-hop. He chirped gleefully in such a tone that I can compare it only with a rooster crowing. He had pleased me and he seemed to know he had pleased me. He had pleased himself, and he appeared to be very proud. We were proud of each other.

Slowly I turned my hand over. His toes, around my forefinger, followed the turn. The forefinger was now the bottom rung of the ladder. He knew immediately what I wanted him to do. He climbed up the finger-ladder. Again when he reached the top, he chirped at the top of his voice. I doubt that any mountain climber ever felt more pride in the accomplishment of his efforts than Fabulous showed those first two times he reached the top of the finger-ladder.

It was a pleasure to hear the cheerful sounds of his chirping. It was a pleasure to watch him learn, and I believe that Fabulous was eager to learn.

The apartment became his.

The first thing I would do when I got up each morning was to let Fabulous out of his cage. He would come out onto what I called his door-porch; I would hold my forefinger near him and he would hop upon it.

That finger became his. Often he leaned his head down caressed my finger with his beak. I felt he was kissing me.

I shall never forget the first day he saw himself in a mirror. He was perched on my finger, and I was holding him close to my cheek; I took him into the bathroom, and stood in front of the medicine cabinet mirror. There was excitement as well as trills in his tone. He fluttered his wings; there were indications of excitement in his action. At first, I believe he thought there was another bird in the mirror. His neck stretched out toward that bird in the mirror, so I stood closer and tapped the surface of the mirror with my finger. He tapped the mirror with his beak. He looked at me, then at my reflection in the mirror. He looked at and pecked at his own reflection. He looked amazed.

I am sure he soon learned that what he saw in the mirror was not another bird, but a reflection of his own beautiful self. He would cock his head from side to side, and joyfully chirp as he saw his reflection do the same. He would flip around on my finger and look over his shoulder at his reflection. Fabulous appeared to be exquisitely vain.

While I was getting dressed to go to work each morning, Fabulous would be on my head or on my shoulders or on my fingers. He learned to hop from one part of me to another as I put on my clothes, hopping out of the way or onto each article of clothing. One of the last things I do before going out is to put on my tie; one of the first things I do when I come home is to take off the tie. Fabulous went through a period of pecking at

the tie and pecking at my fingers while I was
tying the tie. Was he trying to keep me from
going out and leaving him?

In any case, pecking at the tie could not prevent me from going out, so he adjusted himself.
Home from work, after taking off my tie, I would
let him perch on it, and I would swing him back
and forth. He would sing with the swinging, and
the feathers on top of his head would fluff up in
thrilling excitement.

The tie-game led to another game. Holding one
end of the cord of the Venetian blinds, I held my
finger, with Fabulous perched on it, next to the
cord. He put one foot on the cord and touched it
with his beak. He immediately took his foot off
and stepped back onto my finger. The finger was
firm and familiar, the cord was not. So I held the
cord more tautly and encouraged him to step
upon it. Kissing sounds continued to be my best
means of encouragement. He kept one eye on me
and one eye on the cord as I let the cord touch his
front. Testing it, he put one foot on the cord, his
toes wrapping around it; then bravely, daringly,
he put the other foot on the cord. I removed the
hand on which he had been perched; he looked
around and saw the hand was gone. He flew to
the top of my head. However, after two or three
efforts he realized he was safe on the cord. He
walked the tightrope, and as I laughed in my
pleasure with him, he chirped and chirped and
chirped.

After he had thoroughly learned tightrope
walking, one evening while he was on the center

of the cord, I let it slacken, making a swing of it. I swung him back and forth, wide and high. It was a toss-up as to who enjoyed that swinging most, Fabulous or me. This was even a better swing than one of my ties, and his singing chirps rang out beautifully while he held his head high with his head feathers fluffed up, crowning his delight.

Fabulous made a game of life; he made happiness of life. He would take such a simple thing as an empty book of matches and have a ball with it. He would hold it between his beak and push it back and forth across a wooden bookshelf in my foyer. Then he would fling the empty match book down to the floor, cock his head and watch it fall. *"Chirp!"* He would give me a look that clearly said, "Pick it up and let me fling it down again." Of course I did as those glittering black eyes told me to do. He could wear me out as I stooped down and picked it up, stooped down and picked it up. He seemed to receive the same thrill in playing with a paper clip. He would pick up the clip with his beak, hold it high, and run from one end of the five-foot book shelf to the other before flinging it to the floor.

I bought him another toy, a rocking-horse with a tiny bell in the center. He went at that bell from all angles. In time to come he chewed the bell loose and it fell to the floor. He was not pleased with the falling of the bell. He hung his head down. Did he know he had broken his toy? I comforted him and told him I would buy him another one. But the local pet shop had sold out of rocking-horses. I went to several pet shops and could not find a rocking-horse. I had not thrown away the broken toy nor the bell, so I re-attached the bell with a paper clip. Fabulous watched me. When I gave him the repaired toy to play with, he liked it better than ever. His feathers seemed to tingle with thrills.

Still that bell-ladder was his favorite toy. Anytime I was ready to go out, if he was ever hesitant about going into his cage, all I had to do was reach my hand inside his cage and ring the bell, and in he would go, dashing up to his bell. Sometimes he would ring the bell with his open foot, other times he would double up his foot into a tiny fist and punch it rapidly like a boxer punching a punching bag. Still other times he would take a lower part of the bell between his beak and shake his head, wildly ringing the bell. I could take the ladder out of his cage, hold the bottom rung near him, and he would dash up to the top of his ladder and ring his bell. Sometimes he would climb upon the thin wire that curved up and hold the bell. This was his idea. It would not have occured to me to teach him to perch on such a thin wire. The first time I saw him attempt this, it did not work. He fell off the wire, and turning a somersault, he fell to the floor. My heart lept. I was frightened, but he wasn't the least bit frightened or hurt. Before I had time to stoop down and help him up, he flew up like a helicopter and was again trying to perch upon the curved wire. After three or four efforts, he made it. Thereafter, whenever he wanted to perch upon that wire, even though it was a tedious job, he could do so without falling. I have seen him perch there, preening his shoulder feathers, then holding his head up he would sing as though he were singing: I'm perching on top of the world.

It amazed me how much that bird loved life.

CHAPTER FOUR

SOMETHING REALLY ALIVE!

Can a pet teach you anything? Could a pet possibly teach me anything? There was certainly a time when I thought definitely not! But that was the time before Fabulous.

I was in my late thirties when I bought Fabulous. I had not owned a pet since I was a child, living with my family in Alabama. We always had a dog, and I was fond of whichever dog we had, but it was my mother who fed the dog and gave it whatever care it needed. I had simply played with it. There's a difference.

Living alone, a bachelor on Long Island, I learned from Fabulous that I had something alive to come home to, a living being to care for, something really alive! That ounce and a half of heaven caused a lot of lonely hell to fly out of my life. I became one of those people (and I am damned proud to admit it) who often wraps his life around his pet.

I fell in love with Fabulous; I swear he fell in love with me. We truly loved each other.

Fabulous, fabulous . . .

One Saturday afternoon, shortly after I had begun letting Fabulous have the run of the apartment, I let him out of his cage while I went out to do my grocery shopping. For some reason unknown to me, he had never flown near my front door. Since I would be out for only a short while, I thought it would be safe to leave him free in the apartment. However, when I came in with my groceries, my front door was stuck. Unlocking the door, I had to shove and push to get it open.

The sound attracted Fabulous and when the door opened, out he flew, up and over my head, and up the stairway to the floor above. It was a very hot day but I think my heart froze. I sat the bag of groceries down in the foyer, propping the door open with them. I rushed into the living room and got his cage and ran with it up the stairs. As I came to the floor above, someone came out of the apartment just over mine, saying, "Here's someone's canary." Of course it was my parakeet, perched upon his finger. They had left their front door and their windows open to bring in a little fresh air. Fabulous had flown down their foyer and turned into their living room, probably thinking he was flying in the direction of his cage, since their apartment was laid out the same as mine. And there the people caught him. If he had flown straight through into their kitchen where the windows were wide open, he would have flown out and been lost to me. However, when he saw his cage, he stretched his neck out toward it; I tapped his bell-ladder and he hopped inside. He was obviously excited, but terribly frightened by his little escapade into unfamiliar territory.

Once inside our apartment, he soon calmed down. But I was upset for the rest of the day.

Fabulous had very keen ears. Coming home, when I put my key in the lock, even before opening my door, I heard a welcoming chirp from inside. His cage was in the living room, which is at the end of my sixteen foot foyer. Several times, after stepping off the elevator, as quietly as possible, I placed the key in the lock—invariably he heard me; invariably I heard a welcoming chirp. As I walked down the foyer toward him, the welcoming chirps increased: *"Chirp-chirp-chirp-chirp!"*—a parakeet chatter that seemed to be saying, in his own language: "He's home! He's home! He's come home to play with me."

He would perch on my finger and I would swing my arm back and forth as he sang; his head held high.

Often I asked myself, how did I manage to live alone without a pet? How did I manage to live without Fabulous?—such a bubbling bit of life. His energy, his activity, his liveliness amazed me. There seemed to be a ton of energy in that ounce and a half of bird.

Non-bird owners with whom I have talked think the first thing a bird wants to do when it is let out of a cage is to take flight. Not Fabulous. The first thing Fabulous would do was to hop upon my finger and kiss my finger. The gazes he gave me made me know how happy he was to see me.

He stayed on me while I took off the clothes I wore to work and changed into some old clothes. I sat on the side of my bed while I took off my shoes and put on my house slippers. Fabulous would hop from one of my knees to the other, watching me make the change. He enjoyed watching every move I made. He must have looked upon me as some sort of god, while I looked upon him as some sort of angel.

I have wondered why classic artists, all
through the ages, were inspired to paint angels
with wings? Surely it must have been the birds
who inspired the artists. And surely in our war-
torn world, in a world where so much hate runs
riot, the birds are the closest living creatures to
angels that we have.

Whenever we went into a dark room, Fabulous
would watch me as I flipped on the light switch,
then he would look at the light and he would look
at me. I had brought the light. Everyday ordinary
activities delighted him.

He loved the sound of running water. If he was
not already with me when I turned on the faucet
in the kitchen or bathroom, he would come flying
in like a little jet, light on top of my head, and
chirpingly sing with wild joy.

There were times when I had a bit of a problem
about taking a shower. Fabulous wanted to go in
with me. I knew that would be dangerous for a
bird. I would start into the bathroom and Fabulous would follow me, lighting on top of my
head. Sometimes he beat me into the bathroom;
he would perch on top of the glass enclosed
shower, cock his head over his shoulder at me as
if to say, "Let me stay with you and the beautiful
running water." I would lift my forefinger to
him, and he would hop upon the finger. Taking
him back into the living room, I sat him on the
door of his cage or on top of his cage. Before I
could return to the bathroom, like a streak of
feathered lightening, he was back with me. However, after three or four efforts, he would reluc-

tantly stay on his cage while I took a shower. The first thing I did after my shower was to dry the chrome top of the shower enclosure, because I knew that as soon as I opened the bathroom door, Fabulous would fly in and light on top of the enclosure. When he saw me drying myself, he invariably began to preen himself.

Sometimes, while he was eating or playing with his bell-ladder, I could slip into the shower without his seeing me. One of those times I forgot to close the door of the bathroom. The water was coming down on me, not too hot, just warm, and not to swiftly, when suddenly I had a feeling I was not alone. I looked up and there was Fabulous, perched upon the shower enclosure, watching me, absolutely fascinated by all that water streaming down. I told him to go back to his cage. Instead, at the sound of my voice, he flew over to me. The water knocked him down to the bottom of the tub. Quickly, I put my hand under him and lifted him up. He was thoroughly wet and shocked. I was thoroughly frightened. I held the trembling bird cupped between the palms of my hands, and with my elbow I slid open the door of the shower. Dripping wet, I went into the living room and sat with him until he calmed down, which took only a few minutes. He let me know by his movements in the cup of my palms that he wanted to go into his cage. I sat him on his door-porch and he went inside. He was no longer frightened, but he certainly looked a bit perturbed, annoyed that all those beautiful feathers were wet, and now not so beautiful. I got his cage cover from a closet in the foyer; at the same time, grabbing a towel. I placed the cover around his cage, leaving a slight opening so I could watch him while I stood there in the living room drying myself. After about twenty minutes he began preening himself. In another ten or fifteen minutes he was thoroughly dry and he demanded to be let out. It was not yet bedtime and he was in the mood to play. He was all right. I was not all right until the next morning when I took a look at him and saw that he was his usual lively, fluttering, bubbling, chirping self.

Any time anything upset us, he recovered much sooner than I did.

I never again forgot to close the door before turning on the shower, but he frequently continued to try to get in there with me. If I could do it, why couldn't he?

Perched on the forefinger of my left hand, he was fascinated as he watched me shave. He gazed at my face as I applied the shaving cream; each movement of the razor, removing the shaving cream and beard, held his attention.

When I brushed my teeth, he frequently hopped upon the toothbrush, catching a free ride, and chirping away like mad.

Fabulous was mad about life, wild about life, and I often said, "I'm wild about my tame bird." We were wild about each other.

I could be in another room, whistle for him, and, as a dog will bark and come running when you whistle for him, Fabulous would whistle back and come flying, light on top of my head, prance around in my hair until I lifted my finger to him. Then he would hop upon my finger and I would hold him near my face as he gazed at me with glowing eyes.

Fabulous was a singer. He loved the sound of his voice; he had a right to love it—it was beautiful.

One evening I put on "Il Trovatore," recorded by Renata Tebaldi and Mario del Monico. Fabulous sang all the way through the complete opera. When the music paused while a record changed, Fabulous paused, cocked his head in the direction of the hi-fi set, and when the music came on again, Fabulous immediately sang again. It was obviously his favorite opera. When I played other opera recordings, he would sing along through parts of them; he would sing along with only bits and pieces of a Wagner recording, but I heard him sing all the way through "Il Trovatore" at least five times. I think he loved what may be called "the Verdi bounce," a particular rhythm of that opera caught his fancy.

I would have taken Fabulous with me to the opera if I thought I could have gotten away with it. I believe he would have enjoyed it.

I remember the first time I saw the fountain at Lincoln Center. I was immensely impressed and I stood there wishing Fabulous could see it. There seems to be something musical about a fountain, something musical about running water, something of nature's music. Maybe that is why Fabulous was always thrilled by the sound of running water.

Fabulous ignored television. It might as well have not existed for all he cared. Only twice in his life did he ever stare at the television screen; that was when something went wrong with the picture and those awful lines came dashing across the screen. He was on my finger and I got up to adjust the set; as soon as the picture came back on the screen, he flipped around, turning his back to the television. All television critics will admire his taste.

I do a great deal of reading; before I acquired Fabulous books were my best friends. Fabulous was quite content sitting on top of a book while I was reading. Usually he would sit there just looking at me, sometimes he would preen himself. He learned to lift one foot, then the other, as I turned a page.

We learned each other's habits, our likes and dislikes. At eleven o'clock in the evening he was ready for sleep; he would go to a particular spot in his cage which he had chosen as his sleeping-perch. If I happened to want to stay up a little later and watch the eleven o'clock news on television, he seemed slightly annoyed. There was an obviously annoyed tone to his chirp—quick, sharp, staccato; he would shift from one foot to the other; he would stare at me, and those eyes clearly said, "It's time to go to sleep. Put on my cage cover." So I usually did not watch the eleven o'clock news. After putting on his cage cover, if

I happened to step out of the room without first turning off the light, he would be patient for about one minute, then a loud *"Chirp!"* would come forth, reminding me to turn out the light. He never liked being in a dark room except at bedtime, then it was a necessity. I always left a light burning for him while I was at work or out in the evening.

CHAPTER FIVE

SWINGING AND SINGING

It was shortly after I had first shown Fabulous his reflection in the bathroom mirror that I bought him a mirror of his own. It was a polished tin mirror with a chain at the top and a bell at the bottom. No child at Christmas time could be more delighted with a toy than was Fabulous. He was on my shoulder while I washed the toy under the kitchen faucet. He heard the bell ringing, he heard the water running. Double delight! He pranced about on my shoulders, from one shoulder to the other, looking down at the bell-mirror, then looking at me. Gurgling-cooing sounds came from his throat, something like a pigeon cooing, though softer and to my ears sweeter, and the coos were intermingled with chirps. As I was drying the bell and the mirror, he walked down my arm to my elbow, then up my forearm to my hand and onto my finger. As I held the mirror close to him, he repeatedly kissed the mirror; he kissed my fingers holding the mirror; he held a bit of the bottom of the bell between his beak and shook it, ringing the bell; all the while his gurgling-cooing sounds were intermingled with chirps. Now and then he would look up at me, then kiss my finger again.

No one could say "Thank you" more beautifully than Fabulous saying "Thank you" in unspoken words. He said it with joy and love.

Later, when I began to teach Fabulous to talk, I never gave a thought to teaching him to say "Thank you." He always knew just how to express it.

During his lifetime Fabulous gave me very few pecks or bites, but I received several when I was teaching him to let me kiss his beak. It was not exactly easy for me to learn how to adjust my lips to Fabulous' beak, nor was it easy for Fabulous to learn to adjust his beak to my lips.

With my young friend perched on my finger, I leaned my head close to his beak. He drew his head back and glared at me. I leaned my head closer. He pecked me on my lip, and I found out that his beak was sharper than I thought. He did not bring blood with my attempted kiss, but he did break the skin. However, I refrained from yelling out. That would have frightened the bird. (I had already learned, a week or so before, not to yell at anything he did. That was one day when I was leaning my head back, looking up at him while he was flying overhead. Fabulous decided to light, and he decided to light right smack on my nose, his toenails going inside my nostrils. That hurt. I yelled. Fabulous never again lit on my nose or in my nostrils.) Now with the peck at my attempted kiss, I told him not to hurt me. He sat his head to one side, looking at me out of one eye. Then I leaned my head close to him again and tried to kiss his beak. Instead I received another sharp peck. Fabulous chirped in such a tone, a soft tone, that might be interpreted as saying, "I'm sorry. But watch what you are doing." He hung his head down.

I waited a few minutes and tried to think through this situation. If I were a tiny bird, and a great big creature the size of a human being, even a slender person like myself, leaned his head over my head, what would I, a bird, do? What would I think? How would I feel? I don't suppose I would like it. When I had kissed him on his wing, I was down on my hands and knees, and to his side, not towering over him.

I leaned back in my lounge chair, and holding Fabulous up on my finger, I slowly drew him down toward me while I made soft kissing sounds. I drew him to my face and brought him to my lips. Thus, he was coming toward me, not my head going toward him. He turned his head aside; I kissed him on his neck, just above his heart. I could see him peering down at me. Slowly I turned my finger in such a way that his beak touched my lips. Quietly he let his beak rest between my lips. Then I held him up a few inches over me. The way he looked down at me! That look which seemed to say, "Maybe I like it, maybe I don't. Maybe I'll let you, maybe I won't."

I laughed. So far the thrill was one-sided; nevertheless, I was decidedly thrilled. He sensed this through my coaxing and through my laughter. I quieted my laughter; I drew him close to my lips again. He did not turn his head away, he let his beak rest between my lips as I made the soft kissing sounds that he had already learned to like.

We were lovers.

Strange?

Perhaps.

Let Freud come in and take a psychological look if he wishes. I don't care. I don't mind. Love is love and happiness is happiness wherever, whatever and with whomever you find it.

Was Fabulous my pseudo-lover? Was he the manifestation of a repressed paternal desire? Was he my unborn son?

It doesn't matter.

That bird Fabulous was a fabulous, living, loving doll.

I knew the sound of love in the flutter of his wings as he flew toward me; I knew the sound of it in his singing and chirping. I knew the footsteps of love as he lit on my head, as he walked around my shoulders, his beak guiding him by my collar as he went from one shoulder to another; as he walked down my arm and on my fingers. I knew the glittering gazes of love as his black-diamond eyes shone in my direction, whatever move I made.

Freud? go take a bow somewhere else, go take a bow at some old beat up couch. We, Fabulous and I, we were living it up.

Yes, it is strange how close you can grow to a pet. It was strange to me. It was new to me. But there are those who have shared a close relation with a pet and they will say, "There is nothing strange about it at all. It is nature." I also agree with them.

Fabulous did not take me out of the world of literature and opera, he added to that world. Fabulous caused me to wonder if human beings would have ever learned to sing if they had not first heard the birds singing. I cannot compare airplanes with birds, although the inventors were

obviously inspired by the birds. Our planes make
a terrible noise. Perhaps someday someone will
invent a motor that will chirp and sing instead of
roaring like a thousand bulls.

This beautiful bit of flying nature—Fabulous
—taught me to care more about nature in gen-
eral. As I walked through the courtyard of my
apartment house, I heard with a new ear the
chirping of the sparrows and the cooing of the
pigeons. The grass was greener and the trees
were more alive.

Fabulous did not often take a bath, usually he
kept himself clean by proudly preening himself.

I bought him a small bathtub. He consented to
hop upon the rim of the tub and take a drink from
it, but he never once took a bath in that tub. One
day while browsing in a petshop in Manhattan,
I saw a bathhouse for birds. The sides and the
back were clear plastic; the top was red and the
bottom was yellow; the front was completely
open. At the inside back of the bathhouse there
was a small mirror, directly above the mirror
there was an opening just big enough for a tiny
bell that could be rung from inside or from the
outside back of the bathhouse.

When I brought it home to Fabulous, I poured
water in about a quarter of an inch deep. I
pointed to the mirror inside and rang the bell for
him. He watched me. I took my hand out, and he
hopped upon the rim of the bathhouse, then
strolled through the water and took a look at
himself in the mirror. He could only see his head,

and apparently he was not fascinated by such a
small mirror. He lifted his head and with his beak
rang the bell. That was all right. He rang the bell
several times. Then he turned around and walked
out through the water without bothering to take
a bath. His tail feathers were wet and his little
backside was moist, but, alas, no bath. He took an
examining stroll around the bathhouse and dis-
covered that he could ring the bell from the outside back of the bathhouse. This fascinated him.
He walked all the way around it again and rang
the bell again. This was fun—I could see the fun
dancing in his eyes. He took another trip around,
ringing the bell as he passed it. Then he ran
around, tapping the bell as he passed. Again and
again he ran madly around his bathhouse, tapping, ringing that bell as he passed it. And in the
years that followed, Fabulous must have made
thousands of such trips, quickly ringing the bell
as he passed.

Later he did occasionally go in and take a bath,
squatting down, bathing his belly feathers, fluttering and spreading his wings, wetting the un-
derside of his wings. However, he was always a
bit sullen after a bath. After all, those beautiful
feathers were wet and when feathers are wet they
are not so beautiful. He would sit quietly until
they began to dry, then he would begin to preen
himself, doll himself up, make himself beautiful
again. The chirping and the singing would start.
Time to take two or three flights around the
room. Time to light on my head and mess up
master's hair. (Who was master?) Time to take a

ride on my finger. (His finger. You can bet he knew it, too.) Time to take a swing on the cord of the Venetian blinds. I could seldom adjust my blinds without him flying over to me and indicating with his chirps and by the way he stretched out his neck, pointing with his beak, that he wanted to swing. Swinging and singing. Having a ball, having a bird ball. How fabulously Fabulous lived!

No matter how tired I might be when I came in from work, he could always bring a smile to my lips.

CHAPTER SIX

HIS FIRST MOLT

Shortly before I had brought Fabulous home to live with me, I bought a rubber plant. I have a very non-green thumb and have never been able to keep a plant alive for very long. Someone had told me that the rubber plant is very strong and I would have no problem keeping it alive. So I tried my luck with it.

One day when Fabulous was about four months old he flew over to the rubber plant and took a stroll around the top of one of its big leaves. He was enchanting, walking around that leaf like a young prince strolling through his palace gardens. (Yes, Fabulous was King of the Roost around this place.) I sat for a while simply observing him, delighted to see him enjoying himself as he pecked around and strolled around. Everything Fabulous liked, and some things he did not like, he had to examine with that beak, the way a small child wishes to put everything in its mouth, as a dog's nose sniffs here and there, that beak was quite an explorer. I moved over to a chair next to the plant to observe him more closely. I saw a white substance, a milky liquid, some sort of juice from the rubber plant near the stem of the leaf on which he was having so much fun. I am not certain that he pecked at it or tasted it. But I became afraid it would not be good for him if he did. I held my finger out to him and he hopped up to me.

I put the rubber plant in the bedroom and later discarded it.

Was it the following day or two or three days later? I do not remember exactly, but I do remem-

ber it was shortly after I saw him taking a beautiful stroll on that leaf that I noticed his droppings
were watery.

I immediately went to the pet shop and bought
a bottle of medicine recommended for diarrhea
and put the prescribed number of drops in his
drinking water. For a few days it helped, occasionally his droppings were not watery. About
the time I thought the medicine was going to cure
him, he began his first molt. The weather grew
hot; it became a terribly hot and humid summer.
His droppings became very watery again, more
so than before his molt began.

Still he chirped and he sang and he played. He
seemed to feel no pain. Even as his molting grew
worse, he held up, and did not act as though he
was sick. Preening himself, he would take a shed-
ding feather and fling it aside, cock his head and
watch it fall or float to the floor. One day I picked
up a primary wing feather and held it close to
him to see what he would do. He reared back his
head, looked angrily at the feather, then stretched
his head forward and grabbed it in his beak and
rather indignantly flung it aside, as if to say, "I'm
through with that. I don't need it anymore. Don't
give it to me again." I followed his wishes.

Little bald spots began to appear here and
there on his body. I could not help but be concerned about him. However, I had heard of a
finch that had shed every one of its feathers, but
continued to play and sing, appearing not to be
the least bit concerned about being stark naked of
feathers. But as Fabulous' molting grew worse,

his droppings became more watery. I do not know if there was any connection, but there seemed to be. The bald spots on his body looked raw, so I bought the recommended ointment to apply to them. Catching Fabulous and holding down his wings while I applied the medicated ointment was not a pleasure for either of us. His chirping, at such times, became a squeal; his feet pushing at my hand, his beak pecking at my finger; his entire being clearly saying, "How dare you hold me in such a way!"

However, immediately after the application of the ointment he was no longer angry with me. He would hop upon my shoulder and chirp.

I telephoned one of the pet hospitals in Manhattan. The woman on the telephone told me that as long as he was lively, energetic, active, there was nothing to worry about. She suggested that I boil his drinking water and of course let it cool before giving it to him. This I did, and continued to do throughout his lifetime.

After talking to someone at a pet hospital I felt better, but there was no change in Fabulous for the next few weeks. Boiling his water did not clear up his diarrhea, but I felt I was doing the right thing by continuing to boil it. Also, the lady in the local pet shop considered it best.

An acquaintance of mine recommended that I limit the bird's drinking water, that is, give him a drink in the morning, a drink when I came in from work, and a drink before going to bed. This I tried. The first morning as I was taking Fabulous' water cup out of his cage he watched me.

That evening when I came in from work and held his cup for him to drink, he drank avidly. I noticed by the evidence of the droppings in his cage that they did not seem to be quite as watery. Perhaps this was a good idea. But the next morning as I started to remove the water cup from his cage, Fabulous hopped over to his cup, cuddled against it and spread one wing over the cup. He gave a pathetic chirp; this indicated to me that he was begging me not to take his water away from him. "Please, Fabulous," I said, "I don't want to do this but I've got to try anything I can to help you." All during the day in my office I could not get out of my mind that pathetic, begging chirp. I could not get out of my mind that wing hovering over the cup.

I called the pet hospital again and this time I asked to speak with a doctor. I had to call back twice before I was able to contact a doctor. I asked her about limiting the bird's water. "Absolutely not," she said. "The bird must have fresh water at all times." I asked her about boiling the water. "It sometimes helps, it sometimes doesn't. It can't do him any harm." I asked her if I should bring the bird in for her to examine. "You may if you wish. But as long as he is active there really isn't much we can do." I thanked her and told her I would wait about bringing the bird to the hospital. He certainly did not act sick.

That evening I gave Fabulous his water cup and never took it away from him again. He drank and he kissed my finger.

Those little bald spots, those watery droppings! How could I help him? What could I do? People told me not to worry about him—he would be all right. It seemed the only thing I could do for him, at this time, was to go on loving him, giving him attention, and playing with him when he was in the mood to play, and he was usually in the mood.

He loved playing with his cage, crawling around it, pecking at it. I had noticed that he had pecked off some of the paint from the cage, and I began to wonder if this had anything to do with causing his diarrhea. The lady in the pet shop said it did not, because the paint was specially treated in such a way so as not to harm the bird.

I tried not to worry about him. Just watching him, even when he wasn't playing, could be a pleasure—tucking his head behind his wing, taking an afternoon nap, taking a drink of water, bobbing his head up and down. Eating his birdseed.

As yet, I had not given Fabulous anything to eat from the table. One day I brought home a package of ice cream. It was a hot Saturday afternoon. While I was putting the ice cream in a bowl, Fabulous flew over and lit on my shoulder. Eager chirps poured out of that little throat. He had smelled the ice cream and he wanted some. I sat down at the table and started to eat the ice cream. Fabulous rapidly walked down my arm toward the bowl, eagerly, hungrily, cooingly chirping.

"No, no. You can't have any ice cream. It's not good for birds," I told him, because I had heard and read that the coldness of ice cream could give a bird a sore throat and could possibly develop into pneumonia.

But Fabulous had not heard or read any such thing. He hopped upon my hand and reached his beak toward the ice cream. I held the bowl away from him. He hopped over onto the rim of the bowl. Quickly, I put my finger under him and held him away from the ice cream before he could get to it. I sat him down on top of his cage and went into the bedroom, barely getting the door closed before he reached it. He perched on a bookshelf in my foyer, just outside my bedroom door. I started to eat the ice cream. Then I heard Fabulous crying for it. (Yes, a bird can cry. A touch of a whine comes into the chirp; it is not a gay sound; the whine-chirp is drawn out into a cry; it is a sad sound.) I could not eat that ice cream. I poured it down the toilet, took Fabulous on my finger, comforted him, and asked him to forgive me. Never again has ice cream been in this apartment.

I attempted to teach him to talk. The cruel belief that to split a bird's tongue will help it to talk or sing better is absolutely false and sadistic. Such an act I could never perform.

I had read that it is easier for a woman than for a man to teach a bird to talk because of the woman's higher and more penetrating tone; the same article stated that a man should speak to the bird in a falsetto tone. So with Fabulous perched on my finger I attempted to teach him to say "Hi there."

He would look at me, he would peer at my mouth as I spoke the words. He liked my falsetto tone of voice. He was studying this situation. He realized there was something I wanted him to do. Several times he opened his beak as though he would speak.

But he never learned to say those two words.

CHAPTER SEVEN

A DROP OF BLOOD

August came. Hot, humid, sticky New York August. Fabulous continued to molt, a very heavy molt. Beautiful blue feathers, white feathers, white touched with black, too many feathers fell.

One Sunday in early August I saw him spread his wings to fly; the flight began;   in mid-flight his body swayed, fluttered; he fell. I held my breath. I could not believe what I saw; it was too painful to believe. Before I could move to him, kneel down and hold my finger out to him, I saw him open his wings, attempt to fly, but he could not fly.

Thank God I was with him. He did not have to bear it alone.

He had landed on his feet, his wings spread. I knelt to him and he hopped upon my finger. I held him pressed warmly against my cheek; I could feel his heart beating rapidly. I talked to him until he calmed down—until I calmed down. I told him he would be all right. He must be all right.

He chirped. It was not exactly a crying chirp, it was a disturbed chirp, a questioning chirp.

A short while later that day I saw a drop of blood in his droppings. I knew this was a danger sign.

I called the pet hospital. On a Sunday evening there was only one doctor on duty and he had gone out to dinner. The lady who answered the telephone said she would have him call me as soon as he came in. I told her it was an emergency.

While waiting for the doctor to call, I knelt

down and prayed, begging God to help Fabulous. I felt helpless, knowing that Fabulous needed help, but not knowing what to do. That pathetic brief chirp he had given at his loss of flight! How would I feel if I lost my ability to walk? Probably he felt even worse. It seems to me that wings are more precious than legs. That drop of blood. It terrified me. I prayed fervently and deeply while waiting for the doctor to return my call. I had to wait for nearly an hour.

Fabulous was not singing, he was not chirping, he was not playing. I heard no bells ringing. He was sitting quietly on one of his perches, looking sad and downcast, as though he was asking himself: "What happened to my wings? Why can't I fly?" That pathetic expression clawed at my heart. I knew I loved him, but I don't think I knew until that moment just how much.

I questioned God as a child might. "Why, God, why must such an innocent thing as a pet suffer? Why, God, why must such an innocent bird be sick?"

I also promised God that if He would let Fabulous get well, let Fabulous fly again, I would always thank Him.

At last, the doctor returned my call. He asked if the bird's feathers were puffed up. They were not. That was a good sign, he told me, because puffed feathers are an indication of serious illness. He encouraged me and he comforted me, and he told me to bring the bird in to Dr. T. as soon as possible. Dr. T. was the doctor whom I had talked with previously. She specialized in birds. I made an appointment for the following day. I would take off from work. In the meantime, he told me, to let the bird rest quietly and to keep him in his cage.

It was not easy for me to close the door on Fabulous that evening. He was used to being out while I was in, except while we were sleeping. I took his cage into the bedroom with me, put on his cover, and went to bed early. I did not sleep well, I was awake silently praying most of the night. Occasionally I heard the flapping of his tail which is sometimes a symptom of diarrhea, but I think he slept fairly well most of the night.

The following morning the first thing I did was to go to the local pet shop and buy a carrying cage. When I brought it home, I placed his rocking-horse in the bottom of the small cage. I held my finger out for Fabulous to hop upon, then held my finger close to the door of the carrying cage. He hopped in without protest. But when I closed the door, he hopped upon the wires of the door, wanting out. He resented being shut up in such a small cage. I punched a few air holes in a shopping bag and put the cage in the bag. Going down in the elevator Fabulous looked up and gave me a questioning-chirp; I answered with kissing sounds to soothe him and told him we must go to the doctor.

Anytime Fabulous gave me what I interpreted to be a questioning-chirp, I always answered him. From my experience and from talking with other pet lovers, I believe there is a certain rapport that builds up between the pet and its owner enabling each instinctively to understand the other, whether in dog language, cat language, bird language, or what have you. There is a communication of love.

I was fortunate in getting a taxi before I had walked two blocks. The day was hot and I did not want to take him on a sultry subway train. Frankly, I thought my bird was too good for the subways. In the taxi Fabulous became aware of the difference in our movement; I heard a questioning-chirp. The shopping bag was in my lap; I opened the top of it and looked inside. Fabulous looked up at me and gave me another questioning-chirp. "We're riding in a taxi, baby. We have to go to the doctor," I whispered to him, and I was slightly embarrassed, talking baby-talk in the presence of the taxi driver. "What have you got in there, buddy?" he asked. "My pet bird. He's sick. I don't know how serious it is, but I have to take him to a doctor." He was understanding— he turned out to be a pet lover, too. "Know how you feel. Got a dog myself. Never had a bird. You say he's a pet?" I told the driver how Fabulous would fly to me whenever I whistled for him, how Fabulous would whistle, how Fabulous greeted me whenever I came home. "I'll be damned," he said. "Never knew a bird could be like that. What seems to be the matter with him?" I told him. "Sure hope he'll be okay," the driver said. "Sure gets at me when my dog gets sick, must get you the same way."

In the waiting room I removed the carrying cage from the shopping bag. Fabulous and I had

to wait for nearly two hours. For a while Fabulous was annoyed at the sounds of the other pets.
There was only one other person in the waiting
room with a bird, which was also a parakeet; she
was sitting on the first row and I was on the fifth
or sixth row. Fabulous and the other bird did not
see each other until the woman had seen the doctor and was on her way out. She paused and
spoke to me, telling me what a beautiful bird I
had. Fabulous enthusiastically hopped over to the
side of his cage, peered up at the other parakeet,
and greeted it with a string of double-chirps:
"Chirp-chirp. Chirp-chirp. Chirp-chirp." As I recall,
the other bird returned only a single chirp. Perhaps he was too sick to be excited or perhaps he
had been with his human companion for so long
he no longer cared very much about his own
kind. Fabulous' eyes followed the lady and the
parakeet as they left.

On the same bench, sitting at the opposite
end, there was a man and his wife, a little girl,
and a big dog. Now and then the big dog
would take a few steps toward Fabulous, back
away, look up at his master or mistress, and
prick up his ears as he heard Fabulous chirp.
The dog did not bark or growl, some sort of
mumbling sounds came from his throat as he
set his head from one side to the other. Hearing these sounds Fabulous would hop upon the
side of his cage in the direction of the dog,
peering inquisitively at the dog. Some sort of
unknown, not quite known, what-in-the-world-
is-this, communication went on between the

bird and the dog. It was nature's communication.

Fabulous gave me his questioning-chirp; I answered, telling him it was a dog, but I did not think I should let him out to play with it. I believe Fabulous would have been delighted to fly over (if he had not lost his ability to fly) and light on the dog's twitching nose.

After a while they each grew tired of their distant communication. Fabulous straddled the triangle of his rocking-horse and his beak played with and rang the tiny bell.

We had been waiting for an hour or more when time began to drag for Fabulous. He would look up at me as if to say, "How long must this go on? I've had enough of this. Let's go home." And he would give me a soft begging chirp. "Just a little while longer," I whispered to him. To distract himself he went back to his rocking-horse and played with the bell, going at it in various positions. Now and then I would stick my finger between the wires of his cage, and he would lift up his head and kiss the tip of my finger.

At long last I heard my name called. Tucking the empty shopping bag under my arm, I carried Fabulous in his cage into the doctor's office. She was a rather attractive woman, somewhere around thirty, slender and gentle. She gazed at Fabulous while I told her about his loss of flight, his watery droppings, and the drop of blood.

"May I take him out of the cage and feel of him?" she asked. "I want to see if the patient has any growths."

"Yes, of course." This was the first time it had occured to me that Fabulous was a "patient."

She opened the cage and put her hand inside. Delicately her fingers closed around Fabulous, and drew him out of the cage. Fabulous squealed only once. It was obvious the doctor was not hurting him but, even if he could not fly, he objected to having his wings held down. For a moment his feet pushed at her hand and his beak pecked at her fingers. Then he was passive and silent as she gently moved her finger over his body, head and neck.

"You are fortunate," she said. "The patient has no growths. Growths sometime require an operation."

I heaved a sigh of relief.

"You have some kind of ointment on him, haven't you?"

"Yes. It was recommended for his bare spots."

"Don't use anymore of the ointment. The bird will peck at it and that may cause his diarrhea to become worse. Spray him with warm water, just plain water, that will help to get rid of the ointment and will help his feathers."

That was logical. The ointment might be all right for birds who did not have diarrhea, but it was not good for Fabulous. "It was foolish of me not to have thought of that."

"You are not a doctor," she politely informed me. "But I am sure you are a great deal of help to the bird. You care about him, that's clear. You love him and that's what he needs most. But I think I may be able to help him, too."

She put Fabulous back in his cage. Turning to a white side-table (the place was immaculate) she removed a slender stick from a jar. Using the stick she took a sample of his droppings from the bottom of the cage and examined it under a microscope.

"He has no infection," she said. "That's another good sign. However, I notice the white part of his droppings are watery, also. The white part is the parakeet's urine; it should be firm like the other. The patient has both bowel and urine watery droppings. Still, that may not be serious. I've known birds to live for years with this condition."

I talked with her about what may have caused it. The rubber plant? The paint he pecked from his cage?

"We can't be sure of the cause. You say you've already disposed of the plant. If there is some doubt in your mind about the cage he has now, then you may wish to buy him one of brass or aluminum."

"Can he be cured?" I asked.

"When the white portion is watery, there usually isn't much we can do. Sometimes nature itself takes care of the condition. However, I advise that you try giving him Kaopectate. Add two full droppers to his drinking water. If the patient refuses to take it, then give him three drops a day, three times a day, with an eyedropper in his beak. I am going to give you some vitamins and minerals to give him, a pinch of each every day. They are in a powdered form. They will help him keep up his strength and energy."

"He seemed shocked when he lost his ability to fly. When will he fly again?"

"When his new coat of feathers begin to grow. Sometimes if a bird sheds a primary feather from one wing and does not shed a like feather from the other wing, it may throw the bird off balance and keep him from being able to fly for a while. That, of course, doesn't always happen. However, I am sure Fabulous will fly again."

I left feeling much better, but Fabulous was tired from being shut up in that small cage for so long. When we arrived home, and he saw the familiar surroundings, he began chirping even before I could let him out. When I opened the door of the carrying cage, he rushed out and attempted to fly. Maybe in his thrill at being home he momentarily forgot that he could not fly, or maybe he simply had to try it again. But he could not go up or even forward, his open wings let him glide down to the floor. Stooping down, holding out my finger to him, he came to me, and again, looking up at me, gave that pathetic, heart-rending, questioning-chirp: "Why can't I fly? I'm a bird. I like to fly. Why can't I fly?"

I kissed him and comforted him and told him he would someday fly again.

I sat him on the door of his regular cage. He hopped in and took a big drink of water and began to eat. I sprinkled a pinch of the vitamins in one side of his seed cup and a pinch of the minerals in the other side. He stepped back, watching me, while I was doing the sprinkling. I noticed, however, that he ate only from the side where I had sprinkled the vitamins. He would have nothing to do with the minerals.

While Fabulous was eating I went to the corner drug store and bought a bottle of Kaopectate and a small eyedropper. When I returned, Fabulous was still eating. I put the prescribed drops in his water. Later, Fabulous went over to the cup for a drink. He paused. He looked at the cloudy water; he must have sniffed it. He put his beak to the water, shook his head and hopped away from his water cup. He looked at me as though I had mistreated him. All evening I observed him closely. He would go to his water cup, look at it, cock his head from side to side, shake his head, then hop away. I wanted to avoid giving him the medicine with an eyedropper if I possibly could. I held the cup near his beak, but he seemed only to moisten his tongue. Maybe he took a small swallow, but he was obviously thirsty and annoyed that he could not have clear water. I could not bear to see such a delicate creature yearn for something so simple as a drink of clear water. I sat beside him debating with myself as to whether or not I should let him wait until he became thirsty enough to drink his medicated water. But he came out onto the door-porch of his cage, gazed at me and gave me such a pleading chirp, I knew I would have to let him have his way.

I stood up and let him hop upon my finger, and taking him into the kitchen, he saw his bathhouse on the center of the table. He stretched his neck out, his beak clearly pointing toward his bathhouse, and uttered short grunting-chirps. While

I held him close to it, he placed one foot on the rim of his bathhouse and leaving his other foot on my finger, he drank to his heart's content. When he placed his foot on my finger again, he said *"Chirp-chirp"* in such a tone that it could only be interpreted as "Thank you. I needed that." Then he kissed my finger.

That beautiful innate sense of appreciation!

If he had not already taken my heart into his feathered bosom, he would have captured it then.

The following day I called Dr. T. and told her Fabulous would not take his minerals or drink his medicated water. She recommended that I keep trying the minerals for a few days and then if he continued to refuse them, not to try any longer. And that is what happened, Fabulous absolutely refused to take his minerals. They were a darker powder, and with his beak he brushed them out of his cup. The doctor told me to give him the Kaopectate with an eyedropper.

I knew that would be a problem—Fabulous would not like it. That evening, before doing so, I sat with him while Eileen Farrell sang "I've Got A Right To Sing The Blues." That was another one of his favorite records.

As tenderly as I could I placed my hand around him, nevertheless, it caught him by surprise. He squealed his objections; his feet pushed at my hand and his beak pecked at my fingers as I made ready to give him the Kaopectate.

Using an eyedropper, trying to get those drops of medicine down the mouth of a bird you love is an excruciating job. Just when I thought I would get a drop between his beak he would turn his head, or when he opened his beak to squeal and I squeezed the dropper, he would clamp his beak shut and flick the drop off and away. Much more of the medicine went onto my hand than into his mouth. For such a small creature he certainly put up a big fight against taking his medicine.

I remembered when I was a child and I remembered my nephews when they were children, squirming and squealing against a dose of medicine, but my mother and my sister continued until they succeeded. I knew I had to succeed.

Through repeated efforts, when Fabulous would open his beak to squeal, I finally managed to get some medicine down him. I could only estimate and hope that I had given him as much as three drops. It was hard to know, because he could hold it back with his tongue, then flick it away—his way of spitting it out.

The next morning he put up the same resistance, except he did not squeal. He let out a sound that I had come to recognize and which I felt sure was his way of expressing grief. It was a sound of crying. This was much worse than hearing him cry that time he sat outside my bedroom door, crying for ice cream. The ice cream we could do without. But he had to have his medicine. There I sat at the table, trying to give him his medicine; Fabulous was crying and my heart was aching.

Even though I put him through the misery of making him take his medicine, I believe he sensed, instinctively knew, I was trying to help him.

Fabulous no longer acted as if he was King of the Roost. He seemed like a bird who has lost its unique ability, its supreme ability, its ability to fly. But he had not lost his will to live. I instinctively knew, I sensed, what a tremendous will to live glowed in that tiny body.

I bought him a new cage, a shining brass cage. He enjoyed his original white house cage so much I was a bit afraid he might not take to a new one. However, as soon as I had washed and dried it, put in the gravel paper and gravel, put in fresh food and water, and hung inside a new swing with bells attached, I held the new cage close to the door of his old cage—he hopped right in and made himself at home. He examined each perch, saw where his food and water was placed, crawled up and down the wires of the cage inspecting and exploring everything about his new home. He rang the bells on the swing and chirped his approval.

I had placed the bell swing near the backside of the cage so he could climb up to it because his wings could no longer lift him up. That night he choose the bell swing as his sleeping perch, and at night he never slept anywhere else.

For sentimental reasons, I did not want to throw away his original cage immediately. I placed it on a side table next to my lounge chair, lowered his cage-stand so the door of his new cage was on a level with the top of his old cage. I called the old cage his playhouse. I bought a double mirror—one side of it was a magnifying mirror—and placed it between the wires of the top of his playhouse where it fit snugly. Mirrors always fascinated Fabulous, and it was interesting to see how much he preferred the magnifying side of the mirror to the regular side. I attached his rocking-horse to the top of his playhouse, leaving the bell-lader and the bell-mirror inside his new home so he could amuse himself while I was away at work. Although he could not fly, it was still necessary to close him in his cage while I was out. If he had attempted to fly, the chances are he would have fallen or glided to the floor and been unable to get back up into his cage to his food and water.

One evening during this time of his illness, Fabulous was busy chattering to himself in the magnifying mirror on top of his playhouse, and he did not immediately notice that I took his new home into the kitchen to clean it at the draining-board. While I was changing the paper in the cage, I heard a pitiful little chirp. Fabulous had glided down from his playhouse and walked into the kitchen to find me and his cage. As I looked down at him on the floor, he was walking in, looking up at me, and giving me such a pleading *"Chirp-chirp"* that I never again took his cage out without giving him the chance to hop upon it and go with me. As soon as I knelt to him he hopped upon my finger, and when I held my finger close to his cage, he hopped inside and was content.

CHAPTER EIGHT

A SONG OF REGAINED FLIGHT

The days and the nights passed and Fabulous was not getting any better. The heavy molting continued through the heat of August; his droppings were still watery. I continued giving him his vitamins and his medicine. Although there were times when he was downcast and blue, there were other times when he would chirp and sing. He played with his bells, but not as vigorously as he had before his illness.

I liked the doctor at the pet hospital and talked with her several times about Fabulous after we had seen her. We kept him on the Kaopectate for a week, took him off it for a week, then put him back on it again. Although her prescriptions helped to keep him alive, helped to keep his condition from getting much worse, he was not cured.

I wanted to consult another doctor. So I telephoned the Audubon Society and they gave me the names of two or three doctors who specialize in birds. One, Dr. F., I telephoned for an appointment. He told me not to bring the bird in a carrying cage but to bring him in his regular cage, the one he used everyday, because, he said, he could learn a lot about the bird by looking at its cage. Also, I was not to clean the cage before bringing the patient.

A friend of mine with a car agreed to drive Fabulous and me to the doctor. His office was far uptown in Manhattan. It was just as dusty and unkept as the pet hospital was immaculately clean. My friend whispered to me, after we walked down a long dimly lit foyer into an unscrubbed waiting room, "This looks more like a place where a woman would come for an abortion than a place to bring a pet." She was a cat lover.

We waited while the doctor took care of a dog, then another dog. We were wondering if this place was good enough for Fabulous, a delicate bird. The doors between the waiting room and the consultation room, which was also the operating room, were left open. The doctor seemed a little strange; several times we heard him roar at the owners of the pets. Yes, we were thinking about leaving, when a couple carried in a large cat which was gasping and had been gasping and unable to eat for the past three days. We saw the doctor take a fluoroscope of the cat. We heard the doctor roar at the couple: "Just as I thought! You let the cat play with a string and on the other end of the string there was a needle. The needle is lodged between the tongue and the roof of the mouth."

"Oh, how terrible," the lady said. "He's always playing with strings. He must have got into my sewing basket. We had no idea what was the matter."

"You want to stay and watch me operate or do you want to go? I've got to get busy."

"Will he be all right?"

"Of course he'll be all right! I said I was going to operate, didn't I? You want to stay or you want to go?"

"We'll go. I couldn't bear to watch. But when can we come back for him?"

"Call me in the morning and I'll let you know. I'm going to give the patient an anesthetic and operate immediately. Let him sleep in peace for a while. When he wakes up he'll be all right. Goodnight. Goodnight."

They left.

My friend and I sat staring at the doctor as he gave the cat an anesthetic, and as he held the cat's head back he reached some sort of medical instrument down the cat's throat, held the cat's tongue down with one. instrument and withdrew the needle with another instrument. At that instant the cat began to gasp for breath. The doctor manipulated the cat's abdomen with smooth and steady manipulations until the cat was breathing easily. He put it to bed in a large cage, turned to us and snapped, "Next patient."

He might be a little strange (as he himself admitted later) but after seeing that successful operation, I thought he must be brilliant.

Taking Fabulous into the doctor's office, my friend followed me. We stopped in our tracks. My friend turned as if she would dash out the door.

"They won't hurt you," the doctor said.

A door was open into another room where we saw two huge birds. The doctor told us they were Macaws. Their feathers were brilliant hues of red and green. But it was their claws and beaks that startled us. I would not have wanted to tussle with either of them, and my friend was afraid they might want to tusstle with her.

"They're loose!" she exclaimed.

"So are you!" the doctor snapped.

I intervened by telling the doctor the condition of Fabulous. While I talked the doctor peered closely at Fabulous and his cage. Fabulous looked up at the doctor as if to say, "I hope you get an eye-full."

"He's still a young bird," the doctor said. "I can see that just by looking at him. How old is he?"

"About seven months."

"Hops around in his cage like he's an active little fellow."

"He's active. But not as active as he was. And he still can't fly. It seems to upset him because he can't fly."

"Of course it does. He's having a heavy molting. Some birds die during their first molding. Most of wild life dies during the first year of life."

I felt my heart sinking. "He's tame," I said, as though that must make a difference. "He isn't going to die, is he? He can't die. I love that bird."

"I didn't say he was going to die. I see no indication of that. He may not feel in top shape, but there is still a lot of life in him. What's that stuff you've got on him?"

"An ointment I bought in the pet shop for the bare spots. Another doctor told me it wasn't good for him and to spray him with warm water. He doesn't like to be sprayed but I think it has helped to remove some of it."

"Then don't spray him if he doesn't want to be sprayed. Have you given him Kaopectate for his diarrhea?"

"Yes, but his droppings are still watery."

"Give it to him for only three more days, then take him off it. It may not be the kind of diarrhea human beings have, probably isn't. While you have the bird in your hand giving him the medicine, massage his feathers with corn starch."

"Corn starch?"

"Corn starch. It's a dry powder. Best thing I know, next to nature, for a bird's feathers. Some people massage their birds twice a year with corn starch even if the birds haven't had a bad molting. Helps to give the feathers a gloss. This little fellow can use it. The dry corn starch will help to remove the ointment; at the same time, it will soothe the bare spots, and liven up his feathers. Massage him three times a day, lightly, very lightly rub it on in the direction the feathers grow, not against the grain of the feathers. After three more days of medication and massages, do not handle the bird any more. If he wants to handle you, hop upon your finger, walk around your shoulders, that's all right."

"He'll be glad of that. He doesn't like to have his wings held down."

Now the doctor talked a blue-streak:

"You wouldn't like your arms held down either. What are they compared with wings. I like birds. I like all animals. Birds, though, birds are my favorite, they are my speciality. I get more dogs and cats in here for treatment than birds. I suppose that's because more people in New York have dogs and cats. But sometimes when a bird gets sick, the damned fool owner doesn't do any-

thing about it. At least you've got sense enough
to try. I'm considered an expert in my field and
maybe I am. Also considered a little strange, been
told I am. What the hell. People say I talk too
rough. Maybe I do, but never to the pet. Good
thing I'm not a doctor for human beings. Ha! As
much as I know about birds, a bird's instinct is
the best guide. I notice your bird likes oats. He
pecks around in his food cup and chooses the oats
as his preference. Saw more of the shells of his
oats on the floor of his cage than shells from his
other seed. He likes the other seed, he likes them,
yes, but it's plain to see which he prefers. You can
buy the whole oats separate. So do that. Put them
in a separate cup for him. Continue to give him
his regular parakeet food and he'll go to whichever cup he's in the mood for. Oats will be good
for this particular bird because his actions tell me
so. Now tell me what food you give him from the
table?"

"I haven't given him any food from the table."

"Let him have what he wants, except greens or
fresh fruits. They're all right sometimes for some
birds, but not this one, may cause his droppings
to become more watery. Don't give him anything
ice cold. Let him walk around your plate if he
wants to, he might find something there to please
him. Now about the watery droppings, the firm
droppings are the so-called ideal droppings, especially for apartment birds. But that doesn't have
to be. I don't say it wouldn't be better for you and
for the bird, but it isn't always a bad sign. If after
three more days of medication, they're not any

better, then I have a feeling his system will adjust to them. Nature's going to do what nature wants to do. Sometimes we can help it, sometimes we can't. He's a sick bird; I'm not trying to tell you he isn't, but he's probably not as worried about his droppings as you are. What he's worried about most is getting in shape to fly again. The corn starch will help. Then when he starts growing a new coat of feathers, I'm sure he'll be ready to fly. The oats and maybe some food from the table will help to build up his strength. Learn what the bird wants and what the bird doesn't want; so far as possible let the bird have his way, so long as you are both reasonable, and I think you will be. Think he will be, too."

On our way home my friend said to me: "I know the doctor said Fabulous will be all right. But that doctor is weird. Fabulous doesn't look well and he can't fly. You've got to face it. What will you do if he does die? Will you buy another pet? A dog or a cat maybe. Birds are so delicate."

"I would buy another parakeet as soon as I could bring myself to do so. On the third day after his death, if I possibly could. I know he's sick and probably sicker than the doctor let me know, but Fabulous is going to get well."

I combined the two doctor's suggestions for treatment, taking from each what I thought would be best for Fabulous, discarding what I thought would not be of help. I no longer sprayed him. For three days, three times a day, I gave him the medication and gently massaged his feathers.

I continued giving him a pinch a day of vitamins for the rest of his life. I bought the whole oats for him and put them in a separate cup next to his regular parakeet food. He was delighted to receive them; for a while he would eat from one cup, then from the other.

I shall never forget our first meal together. I am not a good cook, and do not do much cooking except TV dinners. However, I like the way I cook pork chops. So that evening after broiling two pork chops, heating a can of corn, putting them on my plate with apple sauce and toast, I brought Fabulous in with his cage and sat it next to my plate. He came out onto the door-porch of his cage and watched me for a moment. He was interested.

There is a sound which comes from the parakeet's throat, a difficult sound to describe, something between the buzzing of bees and the grunts of a pig, or maybe it is a bird-tone of purring. It is a sound of eagerness.

As he made these sounds, Fabulous looked at the plate and he looked at me; he saw me putting the food into my mouth. He hopped down from his door-porch to the table. He walked around the plate, walked across the apple sauce and over to the corn. He had himself quite a time nibbling at a grain of corn. It seemed to me he was having too much of a struggle with it because it was too big for his mouth, so I sliced a single grain of corn into four pieces. He glanced at the four tiny pieces and decided they were not for him. He went back to his grain of corn and nibbled. Then he decided to help himself to some pork chop. He put his beak into the meat, pulled and pulled until he had torn off a sliver. He was happy.

When I had eaten the pork chop, with his nib-bling help, down to the bone, Fabulous decided to try the bone. With his beak he tried to pull a sliver of meat from the bone, but the bone moved as he pulled. So he put one foot on the bone, holding it steady, and had as much fun as any dog gnawing at a bone.

Thereafter, whenever I had dinner at home, Fabulous and I had dinner together. On my days off from the office we had breakfast, lunch and dinner together. I have a picture of him perched on the rim of a bowl of corn flakes and milk. He loved corn flakes. Only about once a month did he have the urge for milk, but when that urge came he enjoyed the milk as much as a kitten. Jello was his favorite dessert. I would stir the Jello and while I was stirring it he would bob his head up and down, flutter, and make those sounds of eagerness. He not only liked the taste of Jello, he liked to watch it shimmer.

I began giving him a cracker as a treat when I came in from work. One day I was holding him close to my chin and I took a bite of the cracker, he saw cracker crumbs on my lips, hopped onto the cracker and ate the crumbs. Thereafter, he preferred to eat the cracker crumbs from my lips rather than nibble at the cracker itself. He would look at the cracker, then stretch his neck toward my lips, clearly letting me know what he wanted to do.

In the weeks to come I could see him growing a little stronger. I could see it in the increased vigor as he played with his bells. I could see it in the way he walked around the table and the way he hopped around in his cage. I could hear it in the sound of his chirps.

One day he attempted to fly again, but his wings did not carry him up. He glided down to the floor, looked up at me and gave me a discouraged chirp. I let him hop upon my finger, kissed him and told him not to worry—he was getting stronger and he would fly again.

Another evening I became frightened. He was perched on my finger with his back to me, and underneath his secondary tail feathers, near his vent, I saw something red. My heart thumped. I thought it was a spot of blood. I looked at it more closely and realized it was not a spot of blood but a new primary tail feather, yes, an important new feather was beginning to grow. He had lost both primary tail feathers but now he was growing a new one! I was elated. When I first saw it, it looked like a needle, about an eighth of an inch long, filled with blood. This was the center of the feather; the blood was feeding the feather, and it seemed to grow about an eighth of an inch each day. Every morning and every evening I took a look at that growing feather. It was amazing to watch it gradually fill out, as the red of the blood gradually faded.

The bare spots were beginning to fade. He was growing new feathers all over his body and under his wings. And most important of all—he was growing new wing feathers!

One evening I saw Fabulous go inside his play-house. His toys and magnifying mirror were on top of his playhouse-cage, and he had rarely been inside it since I had bought the new brass cage for him. There was nothing inside his playhouse except a couple of perches and gravel paper. He walked across one of the perches to the inside back of the cage. I do not know why he chose that particular spot, but he climbed to the center wires at the back and, with his feet and beak holding onto the wires, he fluttered his wings. He was exercising his wings. His instinct must have been telling him he must build up the strength of his wings before he again attempted to fly.

Every evening for two weeks he went inside his playhouse and exercised his wings. Each time he exercised, I could see an increase in the vigor of the fluttering wings.

And I shall never forget it—that evening when it happened:

It happened on a Sunday evening, five months after I had first noticed his watery droppings, three months after he had lost his ability to fly. Fabulous came out onto the door-porch of his cage. Looked around the room. He came to the edge of the door-porch. Fluttering his wings, he looked up. He took off and up. He made one broad circle around the room, one flight around. Then he lit on top of his cage. He could fly again!

For one solid hour he sang. He did not sing at the top of his voice; he did not sing too softly. He did not pause for breath—he had marvelous breath control. He sang beautifully and proudly, with his head held high. Yes, he could fly again!

He had been a very sick bird. Not all parakeets lose their ability to fly during their first molt. Fabulous had the misfortune of losing the use of his wings, and the diarrhea had been a bad case. One problem seemed to aggravate the other. Now he was on the road to recovery—an unseen road of wings.

Leaning back in my lounge chair, I sat watching him and listening to that beautiful song of regained flight, and thanked God that Fabulous was well, while tears of joy trickled down my cheeks.

Fabulous and I were happy.

That beautiful song of regained flight shall never fade from my heart.

CHAPTER NINE

HIS FIRST WORDS

Joyously living again, Fabulous used his senses, his instinct. He did not attempt another flight that evening. I did not prevent him from doing so. His own sensibilities caused him to realize he must not over-exert his new strength.

The following evening he flew around the room twice, pausing between the flights, singing, feeling out his regained strength, proudly preening his new feathers. The third evening he made three flights around the room, again pausing between the flights. Then within a few days the number of flights increased until he was flying around in the apartment wherever he wanted to fly, following me into the bedroom, bathroom, or kitchen.

The two doctors had helped him, I had helped him, prayers had helped him, but his own will to live, his own will to fly again, helped him more than anything or anyone, and of course he seemed to give me most of the credit for his recovery. He became more and more affectionate. He peered into my eyes as though he were idolizing me. I was sure he never wanted us to be parted. When I stood up to go out of the room, his wings lifted up and he followed me. While we were having dinner together, he would nibble whatever he wanted from my plate, then he would hop-fly into his cage, get a mouthful of parakeet food, dash back to my plate, and with one foot on the table and another foot on the edge of the plate, holding his head over it, he ate his seed, dropping the shells into my food. I never minded the shells. I enjoyed his enjoyment.

Life was happiness for Fabulous.

As his strength increased, he was filled with overflowing energy. Sometimes he did not know what he wanted most to do—eat, play with one of his toys, or bill and coo with me, so he would dashingly fly from one to the other. There was a ton of pleasure in that ounce and a half of bird.

Yet his droppings continued to be watery for the rest of his life. Apparently his system adjusted to this condition, otherwise, he would not have had such an abundance of energy.

Fabulous enjoyed playing finger-chase. I would tappingly run two fingers across the table; those two slender bird legs would run after the fingers; at the end of the table he would tap my fingers with his beak—he had caught the fingers. Then he would turn around, run across the table while my fingers chased him. Sometimes he would look back over his shoulder to see how close the fingers were; if they were very close he would give out with a squealing-chirp, like a child joyously squealing in a game. When Fabulous reached the end of the table, and my finger gently tapped his beak, that meant it was time for him to chase my fingers again. This could go on and on. My fingers were usually the first to grow tired, not Fabulous.

A few people asked me: "Don't you think you should get a mate for him?" No, I never believed that I should. I think Fabulous felt that I was his mate; he certainly acted satisfied. I believe he would have been terribly jealous if I had brought in another bird.

Whenever I was out, I am certain he adjusted to my absence by playing with his toys and mirrors, eating and sleeping, and singing. Fabulous knew how to adjust, not merely resign himself, but adjust beautifully to every situation. Even when he was sick and could not fly, he would still sometimes sing, ring his bells or hop lovingly onto my finger.

We human beings so often struggle so hard toward tomorrow that we often fail to really live today. Nature, God, instinct, call it what you will, must have instilled within Fabulous while he was only an egg: "Live today for tomorrow you may die." Perhaps he trusted all his tomorrows to me.

People have asked me: "But don't you think he would like his freedom? Don't you think he would like to get outside and fly wherever he wanted to fly?" Perhaps he would have liked to get out and take a flight into the wild blue yonder, but when the time came to eat, play with his toys, or show affection, he would be looking for his home, his cage—he would be looking for me. And I am not even sure he would have wanted to fly outside (not after that time he flew out the door and excitedly frightened himself), because two or three times I took him over to a closed window, pulled back the drapes and raised the blinds; he stretched out his neck, looked out, then quickly flipped around on my finger, ran up my arm, and sat on my shoulder with his back to the big outside world. One glimpse was enough.

His freedom was internal.

While Fabulous was sick I did not specifically attempt to teach him to talk. However, I often told him he was "Pretty pretty pretty." Coming in from work I often asked him: "What are you doing?"

One evening in early December, I was sitting in my chair next to his cage and I thought I heard a sound from him that I had never heard before. Then he began to chatter parakeet chatter, what I call parakeet language. So I thought I must be mistaken. But in a little while I again heard something like an English word. I listened very closely. He was saying *"pret,"* then he paused with his head held slightly down. Again he said *"pret."* Again the pause, then again *"pret."* He was trying, yes, he was trying very hard to say, "Pretty pretty pretty."

So very clearly, slowly, distinctly, I said, "Pretty pretty pretty," hoping he would repeat after me. I paused. I waited. Nothing. Not a word. Not even a chirp. His head was held slightly down as though he was listening. I repeated, "Pretty pretty pretty"—pausing, repeating—over and over again. But that evening he did not attempt to say the words. He listened, obviously intently, obviously wanting to learn. The following morning I repeated the words "Pretty pretty pretty" five or six times before removing and while removing his cage cover. Just before leaving for work and the first thing when I came in from work I repeated the words several times.

It was that evening after dinner, three or four hours after he had last heard me say the words, that Fabulous said very clearly but timidly, *"Pretty pretty pretty."*

I let him know I was proud of him and repeated the words after him, letting him know I had heard him. He did not say the words again that evening, but the next morning, while perched upon my finger and kissing his reflection in the bathroom mirror, Fabulous said, *"Pretty pretty pretty,"* without the least bit of timidity.

Several days later I invited a few friends over for the evening. I let them know that Fabulous was beginning to talk and I was anxious to know if they could understand him as clearly as I could. I was hoping he would speak as soon as they arrived, but time passed and no word from Fabulous. He chirped and he sang, and I swung him on the Venetian blind cord, and showed my friends how he walked the tightrope. Fabulous and I kissed, and there was laughter when Fabulous stretched out his neck for more kisses. But still no word.

One of my friends was a drama student. He wanted to rehearse a dramatic monologue from John Osborne's play, "Luther," which he was to give during his next class. Fabulous went into his cage to have a bite to eat. We were listening silently and attentively to my friend's dramatic rendition, when, half way through the monologue, Fabulous came out onto his door-porch and facing the actor said, *"Pretty pretty pretty."*

That cracked us up with laughter. Fabulous stole the show, and you can bet he knew it too.

At eleven o'clock, his usual bedtime, I tried to

get him to go into his cage. I intended to take him into another room so he could go to sleep. But he refused. He would have none of that. We had guests. He had an audience. He flew to the top of his cage. He did not want to miss a thing. At two o'clock in the morning, after much bell-ringing, singing and playing, he was perched on top of his playhouse, nodding his head, jerking up his head, trying his best to stay awake. As our guests got up to leave, Fabulous hopped over to his bell-ladder and doubling up his foot into a tiny fist, he rang his bell. They paused near him, looking down at him. He stopped the ringing of the bell by opening up his toes and holding the bell still, looked up at the people, and said very softly, *"Pretty."*

When our guests left, Fabulous went into his cage without any encouragement, hopped upon his sleeping-perch, a very tired and very sleepy bird.

After Fabulous had learned to say "Pretty pretty pretty," it was no longer necessary to coach him to say the words. He rarely ever repeated his words directly after me once they became a stable part of his vocabulary. He said them when he wanted to say them. It was I who usually repeated after him.

Now feeling assured that Fabulous was comfortable with the words "Pretty pretty pretty," I began to teach him to say "Whatcha doing?" Three weeks later he attempted to say the phrase. At first, it did not come through clearly. It sounded something like "*Wh do,*" but I was sure he was making an effort. So I said the phrase slowly and distinctly, over and over. His head was slightly lowered, listening, listening. He looked as though he was a bit embarrassed at not having said the phrase correctly. But he did not attempt it again that evening. He waited. He listened. Then the following evening he very clearly said, "*Whatcha doing?*"

This became a pattern in his learning: three weeks before he attempted the new word or phrase; then a faltering attempt at it, after which I would repeat it many times while he listened, without another attempt from him that same evening; then the following evening the new word or phrase would come through clearly.

And proudly! How proud of himself that lovely bird seemed to be—a talking bird! Perhaps he knew I was proud of him.

Love and pride can be beautifully contagious.

It was in January that I taught him to say the most beautiful words in the English language: "*I love you.*" He could speak the words softly, or he could ring them out, however he spoke those words, I knew they came from his heart. Saying "*I love you*" he would often tilt up the word "you," drawing it out: "*I love you-o-o-o,*" singingly, making a song of the words.

Yes, Fabulous made a song of life.

CHAPTER TEN

A WINGED BIT OF HEAVEN

When I told the lady in the pet shop where I had bought him that Fabulous was beginning to talk, she said, "You saved his life and he knows it. Anytime a person does something good for a pet, the pet is going to find some way to show its appreciation."

Another customer was in the pet shop at the same time, and said, "You loved him, so he got well. Most of the time love can do more than anything else toward getting a pet well."

Yes, it had been rough when he was sick, but all in all Fabulous made life easier for me.

There was always something for me to look forward to. Walking the six blocks from the subway station to my apartment, my pace quickened. Fabulous was waiting for me, expecting me, and looking forward to seeing me. When I came in from the office (perhaps aggravated by something in the office, or annoyed by the subway rush) there would be joyful chirps of greeting, a fluttering of feathers, wings would fly to me, and there would be singing and kisses. His singing, talking, playing soothed the troublesome day away.

Fabulous caused me to be a better adjusted person.

Now that he could talk he would tell me he loved me. For a person living alone a talking bird is surely an ideal pet. Of course I knew Fabulous loved me even before he told me, but it's something everybody likes to hear. Thousands of times during his lifetime I heard him say, *"I love you."*

And there were thousands of kisses. Fabulous liked to place the tip of his beak next to my lips and give forth with a singing-whistle for fifteen or twenty minutes at a time. Then he would draw his head back, look up at me and utter a chirp. Somehow I got the idea that he was trying to teach me that particular singing-whistle. So I learned it. Then we would take turns with each other. He would give forth with the singing-whistle; he would pause, and if I did not return it, he would utter a soft chirp—a signal to me that it was my turn; so I would give him my singing-whistle; all this while his beak was next to my lips, singing-whistle-kiss. What loving we loved!

On my days off from the office. I would be in my bedroom with the bedroom door closed, writing the first draft of a manuscript. I could hear Fabulous in another room, talking, singing, playing—making the best of the situation. While writing the first draft of a manuscript, I am usually reclining in bed with my notebook and pencils, having to be quiet and alone, but his sounds from the other room never distracted me. While writing the second draft, which I write with a pen, I am at my desk in the bedroom. During this time I let Fabulous come into the bedroom with me. He would perch on my shoulder and watch me while I wrote. Sometimes he would hop down onto the notebook and peck at the words as I wrote them down, chasing the pen across the page. While typing my third and final draft, Fabulous would sit on my shoulder, nibble at my

ear, or softly chirp and sing with the clicking of
the typewriter. Later when I began the first draft
of another manuscript, Fabulous had taught me
that he could be with me while I was writing and
not distract from my concentration. He seemed
to sense, from my own concentration, that the
first draft is the most difficult, so if he sang or
talked or chirped, he did so very very quietly. I
never in his life shushed him.

I did not teach Fabulous any curse words or
vulgarisms. He was too angelic for such words.

In February he learned to say, *"Kiss me."* He
would fly over to my shoulder, look around toward my lips, and say, *"Kiss me,"* and utter kissing sounds. You can bet I never resisted. He was
absolutely irresistable. Fabulous made my heart
flutter with wings of love about him.

Also in February he learned to say, *"You're so
pretty pretty."* Looking at himself in a mirror,
kissing his reflection, he would joyfully say,
"You're so pretty pretty."

One of my friends, who lives uptown near Fort
Tryon Park, was visiting us one evening; Fabulous perched atop his magnifying mirror and
looking down at his own reflection, said *"You're
so pretty pretty."* My friend said, "That's certainly
an understatement."

Fabulous' vanity was exquisite and lovable. A
human being could not have such vanity without
being somewhat obnoxious. His ego was pure.
Our egos do not know how to be pure, they too
often fail or override us.

Fabulous knew how to flatter my ego. He
would gaze at me and say, *"You're so pretty pretty."*
Coming from anyone else I would have been embarrassed or resented it; coming from Fabulous,
it was a lovable compliment, chirped and seen
through his heart of love.

Anything he liked became *"Pretty pretty."* Nibbling at the tiny bell on his rocking-horse, or
nibbling at the bell in back of his bathhouse, he
would utter *"Pretty pretty"* over and over again.

In March he learned to say, *"Sweet baby."* The
bell and I, his own reflection, the air about him
was often called: *"Sweet baby." "You're so pretty
pretty, baby." "You're a pretty sweet baby."*

Fabulous was now one year old. How much
living he had lived in that single year! He had
lived through an illness. He had lived over and
above a three month loss of flight. He had lived
love, flew into my heart and perched perma-
nently within.

He had learned twelve words of the English
language.

In April, that was our first anniversary, he
learned to say, *"My name is Fabulous."*

Shortly after I bought him, and was singing his
praises to someone in an office, I was told that
Fabulous was too big a name for a little bird. I
never thought so, it fit his appearance and it fit his
personality. And apparently he did not think it
was too big for him—he learned to say his name
and say it beautifully. Often he would draw out
the last syllable of his name, let it ring out long

and high: *"My name is Fabu-lous!"* Announcing to
the world, if the world could only hear, the pride
of a bird.

Variations of his phrases occurred, sometimes
through my teaching, sometimes through his
own shifting around of the words. I often said to
him, "You're a pretty sweet baby," but it was he
who first said, *"Pretty sweet baby is Fabu-lous!"* If
I had taught him the phrase I would have taught
him to say, "Fabulous is a pretty sweet baby."
But the way he said it!—grammar be damned—
I preferred his way, and did not correct him.

Only two or three times in his life did he say,
"My name is Fabbie. " I did not like that name, so
I corrected him. One of those times he looked
over his shoulder with a slight scowl on his face;
another time he lowered his head as though he
were ashamed.

He would speak his words in different tones. I
remember the time (this was after he had grown
adjusted to my ties) when I came in from work
too tired immediately to change into old clothes,
and in the mood for a quick, relaxing drink, I
leaned back in my lounge chair; Fabulous lit on
my belt buckle and slowly crawled up my tie.
About three-fourths of the way up the tie, he
paused and gazing up at me, he said, softly and
caressingly, *"Whatcha doing, baby?"* That got me,
got me right at a heartstring. A massage could not
have been more helpful.

Another time, when he was on top of his cage
on the draining board where I had been cleaning
the cage, I was putting dishes in the dishwasher;

I dropped and broke a glass; Fabulous hopped over to the edge of his cage, glared at the broken glass, and snapped, *"Whatcha doing!"*

Scientist, ornithologist, and others may tell us a talking bird does not know what it is saying. I have heard cat lovers say they know what their cat is saying, so if the cat lover knows, why shouldn't the cat know? And I have heard the same from dog lovers. They may not know what they are saying in the same way we know, they may not know intellectually, they don't need to know intellectually, they know through sensitivity, through instinct, through love.

However, when anyone asked me if Fabulous knew what he was saying, I would tell them: "In that respect, Fabulous is like people. People sometimes know what they are saying, and they sometimes don't know what they are saying, and they sometimes talk just to hear themselves talking. And Fabulous is that way, too."

Fabulous enjoyed learning. If he happened to be perched on my finger with his back to me, even if he was busily engaged in the art of preening, and I began teaching him a new phrase, using the particular tone of voice, he would flip around toward me, stretch his neck toward my mouth, listen and concentrate on the new phrase. He seemed to want to learn.

He kept himself busy: talking, singing, playing. And it was in May that I taught him to say *"Talking, singing, playing."* He had a hard time with the word "singing." The words would come out, *"Talking, sing* (a pause) *sing* (then quickly) *playing.* " So I would repeat over and over again the word "singing." Once he learned the phrase, he would ring it out: *"Talking, singing singing, playing. "*

In time this was worked into phrases he had already learned: *"Whatcha doing, baby? Talking, singing, playing. "* And: *"Talking, singing singing, playing is Fabulous. "*

During the month of May he began to molt again. I was on tenterhooks all during that molting period, hoping and praying to God it would not be a heavy molt, hoping and praying to God he would not again lose his ability to fly. Fortunately that molt and his subsequent molts were moderate. Each spring, usually in May, and each fall, usually in October, Fabulous had a good molt, and grew a smooth new coat of feathers for the summer and winter. Perhaps it was best for him to have two moderate molts a year instead of one molt as is usual with many birds.

I began saving some of the primary and secondary feathers and a few of the smaller feathers. White feathers, blue feathers, black and white feathers. They are in a clear plastic box, too beautiful to throw away, even if he didn't think so. Sometimes he would look at a plucked out feather, glare at it as it floated to the floor, as if to say, "To hell with that old feather. I'll grow me a new one."

What a relief it was to see him through that second molting, not the least bit ill-effected, flying to his heart's content, a winged bit of heaven.

I loved him so much I had to show some of my love to other birds. I began feeding the birds in the courtyard, the sparrows and the pigeons. They learned to recognize me and they began waiting for me. If I happened to leave for work a few minutes early, they might be in the court-yard across the center walkway; I could pause before opening my sack of breadcrumbs, they would see me and fly over to the lawn directly in front of the door where I stood. Every morning I was proud to give breakfast to fifteen or twenty sparrows and ten or fifteen pigeons. They would look up at me and there was surely an expression of gratitude in their eyes.

More than once someone has snapped at me or given me a dirty look for feeding the birds. I did not let their snaps or dirty looks stop me. There are people who believe that birds carry diseases; no doubt some of them do. Some people carry diseases. Our modern air carries diseases. The subways are an underground breeding ground. Automobiles and airplanes crash into thousands of deaths. Birds carry more life than death, more love than disease.

I know of an elderly couple in New Hampshire who feed the wild birds. When the couple go away the birds miss them. When they return in their car, the birds meet them more than a block away from their house, flying to the car, and flying over the car as it drives home and up the driveway. I am convinced that they know the couple love them, therefore, they love the couple.

One day Fabulous saw a pigeon light on the window sill outside my living room window. Fabulous was on top of his cage when he saw the pigeon. He stretched his little neck out at that big pigeon and glared at it for a split second. Then he went into his cage and played with his bell-mirror. I don't think he liked that big bird intruding so close to his own territory.

After taking a flight Fabulous often looked around at me and gave forth with a joyous *"Chirp!"* That chirp sounded as if he meant "Whoopee!" So it was in June that I taught him to say, *"Whoopee!"* Then occasionally when he landed he would say, *"Whoopee!"*—and his twinkling eyes sparkled up the word.

"Baby" was added to "Whoopee." Seeing him run around his bathhouse, peck at the bathhouse bell as he passed, and hearing him say, *"Whoopee, baby,"* was a sheer delight. How he loved that bathhouse bell! It became a sort of ritual with us, before going to sleep at night, for him to go into the kitchen with me when I emptied the bathhouse and put it in a kitchen cabinet. He would kiss the bell goodnight, and mutter soft chirps and words to the bell: *"Sweet pretty baby"*—*"Pretty pretty pretty"*—*"I love you, pretty baby."* He was like a child playing with a doll.

Also in June he learned to say "Precious." He never learned to say that word very well; I suppose I am the only one who knew what he was saying when he tried it. It usually sounded more like *"Prec's"* than "Precious." This bird-clipped word went into a sentence: *"My name is Fabulous, sweet pretty, prec's baby."*

That same month he learned to say, *"Hello, Honey."* Looking at me or looking at his reflection, the words would dance out of his throat: *"Hello, Honey. My name is Fabulous. Whatcha doing, baby? You're a sweet pretty, prec's baby."*

This lonely writer was not so lonely anymore. Fabulous had begun to love-out my loneliness even before he had learned to talk. Now he loved it out, talked it out, and did a mighty good job of kissing it clean away.

It was during his illnesss that I had formed the habit of bringing his cage into the bedroom in the mornings while I had coffee in bed. I did this so I could keep a close observation of him and keep him company before I left for work. Now that he could fly at will, he would fly over to me in bed. *"Hello, Honey. Whatcha doing?"* After the coffee had cooled off, became tepid, he would have two or three swallows before it was time for me to get up and dress for work.

Several times, with his mouth full of seed, Fabulous perched on my shoulder, gave me a coaching grunt-chirp, and when I turned my face close to him, he pushed seed between my lips.

Fabulous would have given me wings if he had known how. He would fly to the top of the record shelves or to the top of the book shelves, and stare down at me as if he wanted me to fly up there with him. Those eyes might have been saying: "Foolish human being. Why don't you grow wings and fly? It's fun to fly." In August I taught him to say, *"Come fly with me."* He never said it very often. I suppose he really knew I could not fly. Sometimes he said, *"Come play with me."* His mannerisms often asked me to play with him. He liked to ring a bell, then pause, glancing at me and giving me a signaling chirp, I would ring the bell, and he would flutter with excitement.

One evening he was running around his bathhouse, which was on the draining board, giving the bell a pecking-ring as he passed it, having a ball, really tuned in more than any hippy could possibly pretend to be. Fabulous ran over to the edge of the draining board, looked up at me, and said, *"Chirp-chirp."* He turned and ran around his bathhouse again, giving the bell a ring as he passed it, ran over to me, and looking up at me again, he said, *"Chirp-chirp."* It was on his third go-around that I caught on. He was having so much fun he wanted me to join him. I ran two fingers of my right hand around the bathhouse, tapped the bell as my fingers passed, and he ran over to my fingers and tapped them with his beak. It was a ringing game of chase he wanted to play. My fingers chased him around the bathhouse and he would tap the bell with his beak as he passed it, then I would tap the bell as my fingers passed it. This would go on until he decided to turn around and chase my fingers, and that would go on for as long as I would let it.

When the telephone rang, Fabulous would go with me, or he would fly ahead of me, perch on a bookshelf above the telephone and wait for me.

He would perch on my shoulder or on my finger while I talked. Several times he spoke on the telephone, *"Pretty pretty pretty. Whatcha doing?"* And the party on the other end of the wire was able to distinguish his words.

Someone once told me that Fabulous spoke with a Southern accent. However, I am not so sure about that. Some people tell me that I speak with a Southern accent, but I cannot hear my own accent, so maybe I could not hear his.

The heat of another July and August passed and Fabulous was well, he was in excellent health. During those two hot months, I had to be careful to keep him away from the draft of the fan. One especially hot day I had stepped out of the living room; when I came back in, Fabulous was standing on the floor in front of the floor-fan with his wings held open, catching the air under his wings. He put up a bit of resistance when I held out my finger for him to perch on, so I rang the bell of his ladder and he flew over to play. I told him it was better for us to be a little too warm than for him to catch cold.

I also had to learn to be careful about closing doors and drawers. That little streak of feathered lightening could fly so fast he might fly into one if it was slammed shut.

I often left the closet door open in my bedroom, for the simple reason that Fabulous had learned to enjoy playing on my tie rack which was attached to the inside of the door. Sometimes he would go inside the closet and play on the coathangers. He could turn practically anything into a game. *"Talking, singing, singing playing."*

When I saw how much he enjoyed playing in my jewel box, I left the box open and on top of my chest of drawers so that he could play there whenever he wished. He liked taking the cuff-links and tie tacks in his beak and shifting them from one compartment of the jewel box to another. He was a miniature weight lifter. He would struggle with a heavy cuff-link, push and pull it over to the edge of the chest of drawers and fling it to the floor, and gleefully chirp. He knew I would pick it up and he could fling it down again.

In September Fabulous learned to say, *"Oh, yes I do,"* and the word "do" was often drawn out: *"do-o-o."* This was added to my favorite phrase, which was also one of his favorites, and became: *"I love you-o-o-o. Oh, yes I do-o-o."*

In October he learned to say, *"Do you love me?"* And then: *"I love you-o-o-o. Oh, yes I do-o-o. Do you love me?"* And I would answer with the same words. Thus, over and over again we expressed our love.

He learned to say: *"I love you-o-o-o. Oh, yes I do-o-o. Do you love me? You're a sweet pretty prec's baby. Do you love me, sweet baby? Kiss me, kiss me."*

His was a song of feathered love, flying to me with words and wings of love, and nibbling kisses with a singing-whistle of love.

Fabulous, Fabulous, that angelic bird of love!

CHAPTER ELEVEN

A KNOWLEDGE OF HAPPINESS

In November Fabulous learned to say *"OK,"* bringing his vocabulary up to thirty-one words. He was less than two years old. But for some reason he did not learn to say any new words until the following May. Maybe it was because we liked the words he knew so well that we concentrated on them, and variations of phrases, and did not give much concentration to new words.

But he was so obviously a happy bird that I taught him then to say, *"Happy, happy bird."* Happiness poured out of Fabulous, flew with him wherever he flew, and perched with him wherever he perched.

Lighting on my collar, he would say, *"Kiss me, baby. Kiss me."*

I would kiss him.

"Happy, happy bird."

Flying to the top of the record shelf as he saw me get up to go over to the record player, he would ask, *"Whatcha doing, baby?"*

"I'm putting on another record." I always answered him when he asked a question. "So we can hear more music."

"Pretty pretty," he would say.

Coincidences? Perhaps. But such things happened so often during his lifetime, I prefer to believe he sensed, most of the time, the meaning of his words and the meaning of my words. There is much knowledge that is superior to intellectual knowledge: knowledge through sensitivity, knowledge through instinct, emotional knowledge, a knowledge of happiness.

"Happy, happy bird."

Do I sing his praises too much? Then that is
because he sang the praises of life more than any
human being I have ever known.

Oh, he could be mischievous, and he could be
a rascal. And he could give me a scare. There was
the time he hopped on my finger just as I opened
a pop-open can of beer. A drop of beer splashed
into his eye. That drop of beer stung. He
scratched at his eye and shook his head for four
or five minutes before he was all right. I was
uneasy for the remainder of the evening and
awoke two or three times during the night, worried about that eye. I was not comfortable until
I took a close look at his eye the next morning and
saw that it was in good condition.

Fabulous liked beer. He wasn't a drinking bird
and I'm not a drinking man, but we liked a drop
or so. And that is all I would let Fabulous have,
only a few drops. He sipped the drops from
around the top edge of a beer can or from a glass.
He would lift his head and smack his lips—par-
don me—beak!

Sherry had too much of a bite for him. There
was the time he took a big bird swallow, and
hung down his head as if it burned his throat. He
was not permitted to have any more Sherry, and
I never permitted him to have iced drinks.

One evening a friend brought over a bottle of
Sparkling Burgundy and a delicious pound cake.
Fabulous had a ball, flitting from the pound cake
to the Sparkling Burgundy. Perched atop a cham-
pagne glass, drinking a toast to happiness, he
gave me those loving looks of gratitude. He had

more than a drop to drink that night, but I stopped him before he could get drunk.

Hearing him talking and singing, my guest said, "You've got quite a thing going there."

Yes, we had "quite a thing going." I had lived so many years alone and without a pet, I was constantly amazed at how much communication, not only through spoken words, but through feelings and mannerisms, could be shared with a pet. Fabulous was a living dream, always ready to share his love and pleasures with me.

When I went out on a Saturday evening to the theatre, opera, or visiting friends, Fabulous always greeted me when I came in. There was the chirping greeting I heard as I put my key in the front door, and when I went into the living room he would hop down from his sleeping-perch, stretch a wing and a leg, stretch the other wing and a leg, then chirpingly ask to be let out of the cage. He was given a cracker as a treat. Although the hour might be late, after he had his cracker crumbs, he would be in the mood to play. I might be sleepy, but he had taken a nap while I was out, and I could not resist his moods. Five or ten minutes of finger-chase would satisfy him, and then, after he had kissed his bathhouse bell goodnight, he would willingly consent to go back to his sleeping-perch.

How do they—the pets we love—make themselves so lovable? I suppose it is because they are so down-to-earth-nature.

They don't care what is in fashion, what is out of fashion; they don't care whether you are rich or poor, beautiful or ugly—give them a little love and they will multiply it for you.

Even as close as we were, Fabulous retained his individuality. Usually he would do as I told him, such as coming to me when I called him or going into his cage when the doorbell rang or when I went out. But if he did not want to do something, that was it, forget it, he would have his own way. When I told him to say something, if he was in the mood to say it he would say it; if he wasn't, he would say what he wanted to say or nothing. When I learned this about him, I did not ask him to speak. I respected his individuality.

I would simply teach him the words or phrases and when he was in the mood, and he was often in a chattering mood, he would talk. When I was alone with him or when he was in another room by himself, he would sometimes speak softly and sometimes at the top of his voice. Usually when we had guests, he spoke softly, seemingly not wanting to compete with the other voices. Some of our guests could distinguish his words, others could not.

Fabulous would not immediately go to a stranger. He had to know someone for an hour or so before he would consent to perch upon some-one else's finger. He was not afraid, he was cautious. He was not nervous, he was alert.

Sometimes he could be daringly brave. One day I was nailing up a curtain rod in the kitchen. He flew in from the living room, lit on my shoulder, and ran up my arm to see what all that noise was about. *"Whatcha doing, baby? Whatcha doing?*

Oh, so pretty. " He cracked me up with laughter. I had to wait a while about nailing up that curtain rod, wait until he went back in his cage, so I could close him off from the hammer. He would have lit on that hammer and taken a dangerous ride if I had let him.

One day he disappeared for a while. We had been in the kitchen but he flew into another room. I was sure he had flown into the bedroom. After a while I called him to come to me and there was no answer. I whistled for him and there was no whistle in return. I went into the bedroom and looked for him. He was not on the wrought-iron bookcase, and he was not playing in the jewel box. I looked around for him and I could not see him anywhere. I even opened the closet door. He was not on the tie-rack nor the coat hangers. Maybe I was mistaken, I said to myself, maybe he didn't fly into the bedroom, maybe he flew into the bathroom. I looked in the bathroom. No Fabulous. I began to get nervous. Where the devil could that little rascal be? He couldn't have possibly flown out. Those windows which were open had screens in them. But I checked the windows to reassure myself. I searched the living room, all the while calling him and whistling for him. I looked in his cage, I looked on his playhouse. I could have sworn I had seen him fly into the bedroom. So I went back into the bedroom. When I had first gone in I had not touched the door, which was three-quarters open. This time I happened to touch the door. Something told me to look behind it. I did.

And there was Fabulous, perched on a pair of my trousers hanging on the back of the door. I am convinced he knew I had been looking for him. He had been playing a game of hide-and-seek. When he saw that I had found him, he gave forth with a chirp of excited glee, flew over to the top of my head, and pulled at my hair.

Yes, he could be a mischievous little rascal when he wanted to be.

He knew he was not supposed to play on the floor or even light on the floor. And it was rare that he ever did. However, one day while I was in the living room, I heard something fall in the kitchen. I knew Fabulous was playing in there, so I went in to see what had happened. He had knocked one of his toys to the floor and had flown down to play with it. When he saw me come in, he looked up at me and backed up a step or two. Shaking my finger at him, I said, "Get up off the floor." "*Ack, ack,*" he chirped, and backed up another step or two. "If you don't come to me, Fabulous, I'm going to get you. Floors are dangerous for little birds." Backing up another step or two, he gave a trilling chirp and "*Ack, ack.*" Here was a game—he seemed to want me to chase him. I got down on my hands and knees. And he shrilled out his chirps and "*Ack, ack*" as he backed away from me. He backed under the table, and when I crawled under the table and held out my finger to him he hopped upon it with a "*Chirp-chirp*" and kissed my finger.

I had never taught Fabulous to say the word "No." He made it clear with his mannerisms, such as turning his head away or backing up and with a sound something like, *"Ack, ack."*

One morning on the subway train there were two ladies seated in front of me. They looked directly at me where I was standing. They looked at each other and surpressed a grin. I had that uncomfortable feeling a man may have when he is looked at in a particular way, that feeling of wondering did I forget to zip up my zipper? As discreetly as I could I let my hand rest on my belt buckle and with my little finger I felt the top of my zipper. Yes, it was zipped up. Then why were they glancing at my trousers, looking at each other trying to surpress their giggles? I was damned uncomfortable. I did not want to be so obvious as to look directly down at myself, that might have attracted even more embarrassing attention. When the train came to my stop at 51st Street and Lexington Avenue, I went up the subway steps, onto the street, stepped out of the way of the scurrying people, leaned over and looked at my trousers. There, caught in my zipper, was a little white feather fluttering in the breeze. I am sure the two ladies were wondering why in the world a feather would be in a man's zipper. Styles may go wild. But that wild?!

(I told a friend of mine about the zipper and the feather. Although she was dying of cancer, she was able to laugh. Hearing laughter from a dying person is something to be cherished. She loved pets, and her cat went mad shortly after her death.)

Fabulous liked my clothes on or off me, and he

would stroll around wherever he pleased.

Leaning back in my lounge chair, and holding my foot up, I would watch Fabulous run down my leg and perch on the toe of my house slipper while I bobbed my foot up and down.

I was always wondering—what else can I do for him, what else could I buy for him that would please him. One day while browsing in a pet shop I saw a large bird cage, brass, built like a split-level house. It was beautiful. The price was $21.00, on sale for $17.95. I did not have that much money on me, nor would I have it until payday. The second bird cage I had bought for him, hardly a year ago, was still in good condition. But the paint was peeling even more from his playhouse. It looked ragged. Certainly it wasn't good enough for such a bird as Fabulous, although he still loved it. I made up this excuse so I could squeeze my budget and buy the split-level house bird cage and not think I was being too extravagant.

After work, payday, I rushed to the pet shop and bought that bird cage. Paying out the money, I said to myself, "Suppose he doesn't like it? If I spend this much money for a new cage and he doesn't like it, I will be making a fool of myself." I really couldn't afford it and he really didn't need it. I simply wanted him to have it.

When I came home and let him out of his cage, he went with me into the kitchen where I began unwrapping the new cage. Before it was completely unwrapped, he hopped onto it, chirping at the top of his voice, *"Pretty pretty pretty. Oh, so pretty.* " He was wild about it. It took me a while to coax him back into his other cage, so I could wash and spray the new one. While he heard the water running, he made quite a commotion, wanting to get out at me and the new cage. As soon as it was dry, I let him out and while I was putting his food and water in the new cage he went in and began his wire-by-wire explorations, examining every nook and corner.

I felt a tinge of sentiment as I threw away the white painted cage, his first home within our home. I transferred his rocking-horse, magnifying mirror, and bell-ladder to the top of his second cage, which was now his playhouse.

As before, he chose the bell-swing as his sleeping-perch for the night.

We were very proud of our new split-level house bird cage.

Fabulous also liked to explore things which were not bought especially for him. One day I bought a large sack of groceries. I had unpacked nearly all the groceries and was putting them away in the cabinets when I heard angry, squeeling chirps and a wild fluttering of feathers. He had perched on the edge of the tall paper bag and peering a little too far inside, he had slipped and fallen to the bottom of the bag. When I put my hand inside the bag, he hopped upon it, ran up my arm to my shoulder and fluffed his feathers, still a little angry at having that fall.

Within two minutes he was over his anger, and nibbling at my ear. He was a *"Happy, happy bird."*

CHAPTER TWELVE

INSTINCTIVE CURIOSITY

In June Fabulous learned to say, *"Talk to me."*

He would dash out to the door-porch of his cage or come over to the edge of his playhouse and say, *"Talk to me. My name is Fabulous, sweet pretty baby."* You can bet I put aside whatever I was doing and talked to him.

Yes, his vocabulary was growing again. In July I taught him to say, *"Gitcha, gitcha."* This went well with our finger-chasing games, and he learned to connect the words with the game. He would come to the edge of the kitchen table, say *"Gitcha, gitcha,"* run around his bathhouse, then back to me and again say, *"Gitcha, gitcha."* So we would have a ball, playing and enjoying the charms of simplicity.

Life flew around me and chirped up my feelings.

"Happy, happy bird. Happy, happy baby."

"Sweet pretty baby is Fabulous."

It was a pleasure to watch him eat. Eating alone can be dull, but sharing my meals with Fabulous was a delight. If I happened to cook something I did not like, Fabulous with his hearty appetite took the drabness out of the meal. Often I asked him, "Is it good?" And in August he learned to say *"Is it good?"* with a tilting tone to the word "good."

I cannot say he ever went so far as to cause me to enjoy housecleaning, but he certainly added a song to it. The first time he heard the roar of the vacuum cleaner he was frightened, and seeing his fear, I took his cage into another room. The second time he heard the vacuum cleaner he was not frightened—he simply stared at the roaring machine, wondering what in the world it could be. In time, he decided to make that roar something worthwhile. He perched on my shoulder and sang along with the roar of the vacuum clearner, acting as though it was some sort of musical instrument being played especially for him.

It was during that summer that I had my apartment painted. I knew the odor of paint was dangerous for a bird, could possibly kill a bird. So I had to figure out some way to have the apartment painted without it being dangerous to Fabulous. I made arrangements with the painter to paint my living room, foyer and kitchen on Friday of one week and to paint the bedroom and bath on the following Friday. He objected, until I told him I had a pet parakeet. Then he consented, because he, too, had a parakeet and knew about the danger of paint odors.

I bought a large roll of masking tape, and closing Fabulous and myself off in the bedroom, I taped the door all the way around, making sure no paint odors would seep through. The painter finished his work by two o'clock. When I heard him leave, I locked Fabulous in his cage, went into the kitchen and turned on the exhaust fan in one window and raised the other window to the top. I placed a portable fan in the living room and raised both windows.

Then taking my lunch with me I went back into the bedroom, retaped the door, and let Fabu-

lous out of his cage. Having grown accustomed to
having the run of the apartment while I was at
home, Fabulous resented the closed door. Frequently he glared at that closed door, and said,
"*Chirp. Chirp-chirp*" in a tone that clearly indicated he wanted to fly into the other rooms.
After all, they were his rooms as much as mine.
If I could go into them, why couldn't he? I tried
to explain the situation to him. He may not have
understood or accepted my explanation, but he
resigned himself to the situation. I stayed in the
bedroom with him most of the time Friday,
Saturday and Sunday, and did not let him fly
through the other rooms until the fifth day. I did
not take his cage back into the living room until
the following Friday when it was time for the
bedroom and bath to be painted. The open windows and exhaust fans had cleared out the odors.

There was not, at that time, a door on my
living room. So I taped up a sheet while the
painter was working in the bedroom and bath.
It looked ridiculous but it helped. As soon as
the painter left, I opened high the windows in
the bedroom and bath, put the fan in the bedroom and closed the door. I slept in the living
room on my couch until the odors were
cleared out of the bedroom and bath.

Thank God that job was over. It was bad
enough to have a painter in before I brought
Fabulous home to live with me, but for his
safety I did not care how much I had to incon-
venience myself.

His life was loving-life. His health was my peace of mind.

Oh, I sometimes jokingly referred to him as "My son, the parakeet." It usually got a laugh, or at least a smile.

How much of a joke was it?

There was more truth in our love than in the love of many lovers. Life is to be lived and loved, and he—nature, feathered-nature, wings of nature, singing-nature—lived and loved every minute of it. Real down-to-earth basic living and living high.

What has man done to cause him to fail to achieve the kind of instinctive happiness that surrounded Fabulous? Man has evolved, and evolved out of and away from peace. Where are his wings? Has he hijacked them and buried them behind the iron curtain of his soul?

When I was a small child I saw a man take an iron rod and beat a whimpering dog to death. I cried and I prayed and I asked God to take the soul of the dog to heaven, even though I had been taught that only man has a soul. I did not believe it then and I do not believe it now.

One of the most beautiful stories I have ever read is Flaubert's "A Simple Heart," in which the soul of the deceased is transposed into a bird. Birds have often captivated the hearts of poets.

Fabulous was the soul of love.

He was a doll, and in October he learned to say, *"You are a doll."*

He was just as proud as I was of his ability to talk, yet if he had never spoken a word in his life,

I would have loved him just as much.

Several months passed before Fabulous learned to say more words or phrases. In the meantime, in January I noticed spots on his beak. I was frightened because I had heard of a bird who had died painfully with cancer of the beak. I called the pet hospital and asked to speak with Dr. T., but Dr. T. was no longer with the hospital. So I asked to speak with a bird specialist. When the doctor came to the telephone, I told him about the spots—there was a spot on each side of the upper part of the bird's beak and a darker spot on the tip of his beak. The doctor told me that it was probably nothing serious and probably had been caused by the bird's playing with his toys, knocking them around with his beak. I asked if I should bring the bird to him for an examination, but he said taking him out in the cold weather would be more dangerous than the spots, to wait until the weather was warm and if the spots had not disappeared, then bring him in for an examination.

Fabulous showed no signs of pain or discomfort, so I waited.

When spring came, the spots were still on his beak, so I took him to the hospital. On my way in the taxi, the driver said the spots were nothing; he had two parakeets, he said, and they had spots on their beaks. The taxi driver thought the spots were an indication of the bird's sex. When I told this to the doctor, he said he did not think so. Examining the bird's beak, he reassured me that

the spots were nothing to worry about. He compared them with the spots that occur on the
fingernail when the finger is hit or the toenail
when the toe is stumped. Fabulous had, no doubt,
felt pain at the time he hit his toys hard enough
to cause the bruise, but he was not feeling any
pain now. And he had probably learned from the
bruise not to hit his toys so hard again.

That trip to the hospital was not necessary for
Fabulous, but it made me feel a lot better.

During my conversation with the doctor I had
referred to Fabulous as "he." The doctor grinned
and said, "He just may be a she." I blinked my
eyes and asked, "Are you sure?" The doctor
looked closer at his cere, and said, "No. I'm not
positive. It's sometimes hard to tell with a parakeet, especially with a harlequin. Maybe it's a he,
maybe it's a she."

So whether or not Fabulous was a male or a
female, I cannot be sure, and it never mattered to
either of us. In certain lights his cere did look
pink; in other lights there was a tint of blue to the
cere.

Fabulous sang beautifully during the fall and
winter. But when spring came there was a difference. He sang even more beautifully and was
even more lively—a little powerhouse of energy.
And in time, the spots on his beak began to fade.

His curiosity never faded.

Usually I made sure never to leave anything on
the stove while Fabulous was in the kitchen
alone. But one day I had a Pyrex boiler of water

on the stove as I was about to make some instant coffee; the telephone rang, and this time Fabulous happened not to go with me to the telephone. When I returned to the kitchen Fabulous was sitting on top of an empty Pyrex boiler next to the pot of boiling water, intently, wonderously, watching the steam rise. He was fascinated.

I was startled, seeing him so close to the fire and the steam. I quickly put my finger under him and lifted him away. *"Pretty pretty,"* he said. *"Pretty pretty. Whatcha doing, baby? Whatcha doing?"* I told him what I was doing: "Taking you away from the stove. You know you are not supposed to go onto the stove." He did know it, and he had rarely ever gone near the stove, but this time, while my back was turned, his curiosity got the best of him.

Sometimes he would fly over to the top of the console hi-fi set, stroll across the top of it and peer down toward the source of the music, wondering about so much beautiful music coming out of that big box.

Fabulous had a "hurry-up" chirp. It was a rapid sound, something like the clicking of the tongue. If he was particulary anxious for a treat, or if I was too slow getting it for him, he would stretch out his neck and utter that "hurry-up" clicking-chirp. "Just a minute," I would say. "Just a minute." And he heard me use this phrase many times. One evening while listening to the phonograph, we were taking turns in ringing the bell of his ladder. The music stopped and I got up

to change the record. Fabulous gave out with his
"hurry-up" clicking-chirp, wanting me to continue playing with him and the bell. "Just a minute," I said, and he repeated, *"Just a minute?"*

That was one of the few times he picked up a
phrase without it's having been specifically
taught to him, and it was one of the few times he
repeated directly after me. It never became one of
his favorite phrases.

He seldom ever paid any attention to the orna-
ments, for some reason they did not stir up his
curiosity, but one day he lit on the head of Mi-
chelangelo's David. He looked so cute there on
top of David's head that I went to the closet in the
foyer and returned with my Kodak. But he had
deserted David's head and left a dropping on David's backside.

The first time I ever took a picture of Fabulous
the small flashbulb frightened him. But after the
first few flashes he ignored the flashbulb. He
looked at me as if he thought I was silly to hold
that thing up in front of my face.

I kept a framed picture of him on my desk in
my office. His beauty never ceased to intrigue me.

There was always something new to be learned
about him. His instinctive curiosity was always
seeking, exploring, examining.

One day while I was washing my wash-and-
wear shirts, the water was running slow and
tepid; Fabulous lit on my shoulder, walked down
my arm, onto my hand, and took a drink from the
running water. Apparently he liked the tempera-
ture of the water. Glancing up at me, then at the

water, he sidled up beside the slender stream of water, fluttered his wings, wetting the feathers of one wing. He uttered soft, gurgling chirps. Oh, yes, he liked it!—so he flipped around and wet the other side. I lowered the pressure of the water, making the stream even more slender. He dashed under the running water, out, then under and out again. I made a cup of the palms of my hands; he squatted down in my palms, fluffing, wetting his chest and belly feathers. He flew onto the draining board, fluffed, then flew onto my hand and under the stream of water again, wetting himself thoroughly, giving himself a delightful shower.

He continued to astonish me; he could even make the washing of clothes less of a task, adding pleasure to my work. I never again saw Fabulous take a bath in his bathhouse, although I poured fresh water in it everyday. He would drink from it, but after his first experience of taking a shower bath under the running water and in the palms of my hands, he would bathe no other way.

In May Fabulous learned to say the word *"Say."* Shortly afterwards, he learned to say, *"Say, huh?"* These words were coupled with other phrases: *"Do you love me? Say, huh? Do you love me?"*—*"Whatcha doing? Say, huh? Whatcha do-ing?"*

During that summer he also learned to say, *"Yes, suh."* And the word was Southern *"suh,"* not "sir."

In October he learned to say, *"That's what you*

are, "which became: *"That's what you are, my sweet pretty baby."* And: *"You're a sweet pretty baby, that's what you are. Do you love me, say, huh? I love you, oh, yes I do. Yes, suh. Happy happy bird. Talking, singing, playing."*

Living! Because he knew how to live.

CHAPTER THIRTEEN

MORE FREEDOM

It was after the Thanksgiving holidays, after the four-day weekend, that Fabulous began to give me a hard time about getting him to go into his cage each morning before I went to work. Every morning for a solid week I had to catch him, some way or another, and put him in his cage. Putting his bell-ladder in the cage and ringing the bell for him no longer did the trick.

I had bought a very light-weight scarf, the sort that women use as headscarfs, which I had used as his cage cover during the summer. To catch him, when he was in that uncooperative mood, I spread the scarf out and dropped it over him, then reached my hand under the scarf for him. Oh, he squealed in angry independence, but not the least bit hurt. He was (I knew) simply doing all he could to get me to prolong that four-day Thanksgiving weekend.

Unfortunately, financial necessities made it impossible for me to comply with his wishes. So I had to think of some way to appease him. I went to the local hardware store and bought a plastic, louvered door of imitation birch, and hired a handyman to attach it to the living room entrance so that I could close the door when I wanted to.

Now Fabulous had the living room to himself whenever I went out. Seeing how well it worked for him, I wished I had thought of it before, but then he had not insisted upon my thinking of a way for him to remain out of his cage while I was at work.

He still loved his cage, but he simply wanted

to go in and out whenever he pleased. He never once tried to sneak out the door while I was closing it.

As time went on, the longer we knew each other, the more affectionate he became.

Yet he knew how to amuse himself when he was alone. Or if I was at home doing something which he did not wish to take part in he would either watch me or amuse himself otherwise. When he was about a year old I had placed two coat hangers in the bathroom on the shower pipe. I had placed a magnifying mirror (another one—he had many mirrors) on a wire coat hanger and I hung a wooden coat hanger in front of the mirror. How he enjoyed perching on that wooden coat hanger and singing to himself in the mirror! How he enjoyed running around the top of the shower enclosure! It was his own private runway. He had his favorite spot on that run-way—it was against the wall where a metal strip attached the glass enclosure to the wall. One day I became curious as to just why that spot was his favorite spot. I had seen him perch and sing there for long periods of time. So I stood upon the toilet seat and examined the top of the metal stripping. It was hollow. Obviously he received an echo or amplification from this hollow metal stripping which his keen hearing appreciated. But whenever he saw me applying shaving cream to my face, he would stop singing over the hollow or he would stop singing to his reflection in the magnifying mirror, fly over to me and gaze in deep interest as he watched me shave.

In finger-training him it had been necessary for me to teach him not to be afraid; once the barriers of fear were overcome, his natural love grew and rose and flew into a living song.

I remember a certain Sunday afternoon, a very special afternoon in my memory. That morning I had worked hard on a manuscript, so about two o'clock I went into the bedroom to take a nap. I had not closed the bedroom door. Just as I was falling asleep, Fabulous lit on my chin, walked across my face, up to my forehead and began playing with my hair. I raised my hand to him and he hopped upon my forefinger; I brought my hand down to my waist where he stayed on my finger for about two seconds. Then he flew onto my chin again, took another stroll across my face, up to my forehead and chirpingly nibbled at my hair. I gave him my forefinger again. After my third effort he remained on my forefinger. An hour later I awoke, and as I was waking up, Fabulous awoke, yawned, stretched one wing and a leg, stretched the other wing and leg, then simultaneously stretched his wings up.

Opera, theatre, books. Can they live up to nature? No, I do not believe they can. They may reflect, they may illuminate; they may be beautiful and powerful. But nature surpasses all man-made creations; nature is more basic, more lasting, more beautiful; nature is more. Let us pray that mankind does not destroy it, for mankind is also beautiful, even beyond his ugliness, and in destroying nature he destroys himself. This is

known to man, known through intellectual
knowledge, yet not known with sufficient instinctive depth of emotional growth.

Time and Fabulous flew along. From October
that year until May the next, he did not learn any
new words. In May I began teaching him to say
the word "beautiful." One evening he said,
"Beauty, beauty," not exactly the word I was
teaching him, but it was good enough. Later,
when the word "beauty" became a comfortable
part of his vocabulary, he learned to say *"Beautiful."*

*"Beauty, beauty, beautiful. Beauty, beautiful Fabu-
lous. Pretty pretty baby. My name is Fabu-lous!
Happy, happy bird."*

That was the extent of his vocabulary—fifty
words. I have heard of a bird who achieved an
eighty-word vocabulary, and another who
achieved a ninety-word vocabulary. Maybe I was
too busy with external living, working, writing,
and internal problems to teach him more, or
maybe Fabulous simply did not want to learn any
more of the English language. However that
might be, he surely enjoyed speaking the words
he knew. He was a lovely chatterbox. His head
was about the size of a thumb, and I could never
understand how he could retain so many words
in such a small brain. Bird-brain? Brilliant-brain!
Weeks might pass when I did not hear him say
certain words, such as, *"You are a doll."* Then
without my re-teaching him, seemingly out of the
clear blue, but out of his own memory, he would
speak the words again.

A day never passed without his saying: *"Pretty pretty bird. My name is Fabulous. I love you. Whatcha doing? Kiss me, kiss me."* These were his favorite words.

In the late summer I obtained a five-week leave of absence from my office so that I could spend more time on the book I was writing. It was an especially hard book to write and I was very involved in it. For two weeks I did not go out except to the mail box downstairs and the corner grocery store. Then one Saturday evening I had dinner with friends and we went to the opera. I came home about one o'clock. When I opened the living room door, Fabulous flew onto my head and gave me his usual greeting of joyful chirps. I happened to glance at his cage and I saw something dark on one of his perches. It was blood, not just a little blood, there were splashes of blood on various parts of his cage. I was frightened, but Fabulous was on my head, chirping cheerfully in the middle of the night as if nothing had happened. I brought him down with my forefinger and looked at him closely. At first, I feared he had been anally bleeding. But, no, thank God, it wasn't that. He had chewed one of his nails down to the tiny blood vessel that runs into the nail. His foot was covered with blood, and his belly feathers, directly above the foot, was splotched with blood. He had drawn his bleeding foot up into his feathers, thereby slowing the flow of blood and soothing the pain which he must have felt when he bit too far down into the nail. He could have bled to death, and although he had lost quite a lot of blood for such a small creature, there was no indication he had lost any energy. I let him eat cracker crumbs from my lips, and he would have been perfectly willing to play a game of finger-chase if I had joined in. I let him kiss his bathhouse bell goodnight, then he kissed me goodnight, and I put him on the door-porch of his cage. He hopped upon his sleeping-perch and was soon asleep.

I could not sleep well that night, so Sunday morning I called the pet hospital and made an appointment with a "bird doctor." I had asked for an appointment with a bird specialist, but the lady on the telephone had hesitated. The doctor whom I had seen previously had left the hospital. The one I saw this time may or may not have known something about birds. He merely glanced at Fabulous and gave me some ointment to put on him if he bit into another blood vessel. If I had had the ointment before Fabulous injured his foot, it would not have done him any good because I was out when it happened, and he, himself, nature, stopped the bleeding. I was annoyed that such a large hospital could not keep a bird specialist on their staff. Anyway, Fabulous was all right. Within a few days he had cleaned the blood spot from his belly feathers.

He was four-and-a-half-years old now, and I think he appreciated my five-week leave of absence as much as I did. In the mornings, quietly sitting on my shoulder while I was writing; in the afternoons, perched on top of whatever book I was reading; in the evenings, billing and cooing and *"Talking, singing, singing, playing is Fabulous."*

When the leave of absence was over, when he saw me getting dressed to go back to work that first Monday morning, he must have known what was happening. He peered at me with a wondering expression in his eyes, as if to ask, "Why do you have to go out? Why can't you stay with me all the time?" But he adjusted to the old schedule better than I did. He sat on the door-porch of his cage, stretched his neck out toward me, but did not attempt to fly out of the room as I closed the louvered door. I cursed the subways and I cursed the job.

Although Fabulous may have felt a bit blue for a while, I am confident he soon amused himself with his toys, his mirrors, and his own beautiful voice, talking and singing.

For each of his birthdays, March 1, and for each of our anniversaries, April 10, I bought him at least one new toy, and of course there had to be something for Christmas. There were times when he almost went wild over a new toy. Some of his mirrors were made of polished tin, with a bell at the bottom of the mirror. Every so often these mirrors had to be replaced, because they spotted easily and became tarnished. I believe it was the third time I had bought him such a mirror, lain it on the kitchen table while I turned to one of the cabinets to get a cracker for him, he flew over to it, hovered over the mirror with gurgling chirps, spread his wings and fluffed in such a way there seemed to be something wildly sexual about his actions. I do not know anything about his repressed or latent sexual desires, but I have a feeling they were generally at rest; that is, I do not believe he was disturbed about not having a mate.

Near his bathhouse on the kitchen table I kept his vanity mirror feeding perch. When Fabulous first saw a three-way reflection of himself he was surprised. He cocked his head first one way, then another, hopped off the perch, then back upon it and kissed each of his three reflections. His vanity was tremendous, yet as simple and natural as nature itself. He knew the art of self-love without the least bit of selfish conceit.

Still, no matter how much he enjoyed gazing at and kissing his own reflection, if I went into another room, he would soon fly after me, perch on my head and sing, often saying: *"Whatcha doing? My name is Fabulous. I love you. Oh, yes, I do. Do you love me sweet pretty prec's baby? Say, huh? Do you love me?"* He was a real winging, singing dream.

I had never thrown away the small carrying-cage which I had used the first time I took him to a doctor. I kept it on the far side of the kitchen table. The top of the small cage folded back and down, serving as another ladder for him. A music box with a mirror was on one side of the cage. He would not hop upon the perch that was attached to the music box, which, when slightly pressed down, would play a few strands of Brahms' Lullaby, but he liked for me to press down the perch, start the music playing, then he would sing to his reflection. *"Pretty pretty bird. That's what you are,*

a sweet pretty baby. Yes, suh. Oh, so pretty pretty. "
Everyday I heard the music of nature.
More and more I appreciated nature.

I had changed my job and was now working in
an office near Central Park South and Fifth Avenue. During lunch I went into the Park and sat
on a bench near the lake, where I ate my sandwich and drank a container of milk, now and
then throwing bits of the sandwich to the sparrows and pigeons and ducks. One day it was rain-
ing when there happened to be a particular mad
rush job that typists sometimes have to cope
with. I worked through my regular lunch hour,
finishing the mad rush job, and did not go out to
lunch until two o'clock. By this time the rain had
stopped. There was hardly anyone in the Park,
and no one had been feeding the birds during the
rain. They were glad to see me. I had a book with
me and I placed a napkin over the book on my
lap. When I unwrapped my sandwich, two pigeons hopped upon the napkin-covered book in
my lap, several other pigeons were cooing around
my ankles. A dozen or more sparrows were fluttering around near me. Four or five ducks came
toward the edge of the lake. Seeing me they knew
they were going to get something to eat. I gave
them half of my sandwich, but there were so
many of them they were obviously still hungry.
I did not do any reading during lunch that day.
I went to a near-by delicatessen and bought a
large loaf of bread, went back to the same bench
in the Park and gave the birds a feast.

I was sitting on one end of the bench; along the back of the same bench, seven or eight sparrows were lined up. I pinched off a good size bird-bite of bread and slowly held it out toward the first sparrow in line. He looked at the bread and he looked at me; again he looked at the bread and he looked at me. He made up his mind, hopped closer to my hand, stretched out his neck and took the bread from between my fingers. I pinched off another bird-bite and held it out to the next sparrow in line. He did not hesitate as long as the first sparrow—he did not need to—he had learned through his experience in watching the first in line. He took the bread from between my fingers and flew away with it. And so on it went that day in the Park, until each sparrow in line had taken bread from between my fingers.

I was delighted to have the wild birds trust me that much. All they needed was a little bread and love.

You don't have to be St. Francis to communicate with the birds. Merely love them.

CHAPTER FOURTEEN

TOO ANGELIC TO KNOW

It was a terrible year for the world. There was war and rumors of war. The hearts of humanity were warring with each other. Hate was on the rampage. Love tried to struggle out from under the blaze of hate. There was starvation at a time when there was no depression. Wealth flourished. Strikes and riots became as common as going to the toilet. Too many people forgot to bathe their hearts. Murder propagated murder. Two of America's great men were assassinated. People wept in remembrance, then the tears stopped flowing; tear-gas and stones took the place of tender tears. People were proclaiming God as being dead, and did not realize their own souls were attempting suicide.

Fabulous was on my finger loving me while I watched these blazes of hate on television, and I said to him: "I'm glad you don't know what's going on in the world, Fabulous. You are too angelic to know about these terrible things."

During that year Fabulous was five years old. I remembered when he was less than a year old —during that long illness when he had lost his ability to fly—I remembered asking God to let Fabulous live, I remembered asking God to let Fabulous fly again. The prayers were answered and everyday I thanked God for Fabulous, and I remembered Fabulous singing his praises to life that first evening he learned to fly again.

When our prayers are answered we know why. Because we ask, because we seek, because we find. When our prayers are not answered we may never know why. Perhaps to test our strength of faith in the beyond. And perhaps in some strange and mysterious way an invisible love is still singing.

No matter what problems exist in the world at large, a human being may achieve some sort of happiness in his own personal life if he knows something about love. I knew Fabulous, a fabulous love. And although worldly problems threw a dark shadow on my life, I could turn to Fabulous or Fabulous would fly to me, and we enjoyed the innocence of life, even in a world of dying innocence. I remember holding him up on my forefinger and telling him he was five years old. He gazed down at me, then threw his head up and sang; took a flight around the room, then lit on my head and played in my hair. I brought him back to my forefinger and kissed him on his beak.

That was a happy day for me and for a *"Happy, happy bird,"* but a few days later I remembered several people had told me that the fifth year of a parakeet's life is a dangerous year—often their respiratory system weakens and they develop a respiratory disease, or something else goes wrong. They may die during this crucial year. I continued my prayers to God, thanking God for Fabulous and asking God to give Fabulous a long life.

During his second, third and fourth years, each year I did not think it was possible for him to become any more affectionate. Yet during his fifth year, his affection, his attention, his love continued to grow. We seemed to have grown into each other. He was a part of me and I knew I was

a part of him. An ounce and a half can be tremendous when it is sincere. With his chest resting on
my chin, I could feel his heart beating on my
flesh; his feathers, softer than the petals of a rose,
were a soothing touch. Anytime I came in, his
feathers fluttered as he took wing and flew to me.
Comparable to a child running to meet the fa-
ther; comparable to a dog hopping up to greet the
master; comparable to a kitten brushing against
the ankles of someone it loves. Fabulous, with his
wings of love, did not let me be out of his sight
whenever it was possible for us to be together.

How beautiful is the unadulterated love of a
pet for its beloved! Never selfish, never hurting
you, just plain down-to-earth heavenly loving
you. How much humanity needs to learn from
these creatures of love! Yes, even an ounce and a
half can go a long, long way.

Yet there are those who are polluting the wa-
ters, polluting the air, polluting the earth, failing
to heed the genius of Rachel Carson. If the birds
should vanish, we shall not be far behind. They
are the forerunners, the foretasters, of the air we
breathe. A glance at the wild birds or the domes-
ticated birds can reveal to anyone how much they
love life.

Birds are the living connecting link between
heaven and earth.

A bullet for a bird is a bullet against nature,
and there is no sportsmanship in the act. Where
have the many eagles gone, where have many
geese gone? They have gone with many blazing

guns and many poisons. Bye-bye blackbird? Bye-bye life.

Now in the fifth year of the life of Fabulous, nature was to take its toll.

(How hard it is to write these words! It has been a pleasure writing about his life, his love, his vitality. The words have flown out and on to my notebook, the very same notebook on which he has strolled across and pecked at the words of other manuscripts I have written. Yet death is a part of life, a slice into our hearts, a part which we cannot pass over, a part which we must face. And I, as a writer, must face all parts of life with the written word, even as Fabulous faced it with his wings and his songs and his chirps.)

It was in May that he caught a cold. It did not seem to be a terribly bad cold. He did not wheeze, his feathers were not ruffled. But he sneezed wet sneezes, softer than the sneezes of a kitten. He continued to play, although I did not encourage him to play when he had the bad cold. I let him do what his nature thought best. I thought about taking him to a doctor, but taking him out in the weather would be taking chances. I gave him Pet-mycin, which had a number of times in the past cleared up his sneezing, cured a bit of a cold, or prevented a cold. It was a good medicine. He had the cold for two weeks, and then there was no further indication of it or any sort of infection. The lessening of his vitality during those two weeks was barely perceptible. Now he was his usual self again, talking and singing at the top of his glorious voice, and playing with as much fun and energy as he had ever known.

In the middle of June, two or three weeks after Fabulous had recovered, I gave a birthday party for a friend. There were present ten people and one bird. Fabulous was the life of the party, and he knew it too. Fortunately he did not go onto the floor even once, although two or three of us were sitting on the floor, which could have been a temptation for him to get down with us. (I had heard of a bird being accidentally crushed to death beneath someone's foot at a party. The lady who owned the bird was so grief stricken she had to go into a hospital for a week after her bird's death.) Fabulous flew from one to another, nibbled the top of someone's nose, walked around the shoulder of someone else, and examined the finger-perch of various ones. He did a lot of chirping and a bit of talking, usually talking softly in the presence of others. He showed them how vigorously he could ring his bells. Someone commented, "He's having a real battle with that bell." How that bird loved his battles with his bells!—shaking them with his beak, doubling up his foot into a tiny fist and ringing away like mad —a tender wilderness of domestic jungle love. Actually even with all the people here, he did not play any more than he would have if we had been alone. He did not exert himself and no one annoyed him in the least. But at eleven o'clock, his usual bedtime, he showed signs of being sleepy.

So I took him with his cage into the bedroom, kissed him goodnight, turned out the light and closed the bedroom door.

I did not think anything about it at the time, but later I wondered why he did not protest about being put to bed while we had guests. I realized he was no longer a young bird, but I did not think he was old. However, later someone said, "I had the feeling he was old for a bird." Had he, an utter stranger to the bird, noticed something about him that I had not noticed?— on-coming age.

The day after the party and the following days, Fabulous was that *"Happy, happy bird"* he made life be, revealing no indication of any ill effects from his bad cold.

The week after the party, I made arrangements to have my apartment painted again, three years had passed since it had been painted. I made the same arrangements of having the living room, foyer and kitchen painted, letting it dry and deodorize for a week, then having the bedroom and bath painted. I took the same precautions about not letting Fabulous into a room where there were any odors of paint. He was not as upset about being closed off in the bedroom as he had been before. Did he remember that paint job three years ago? I don't know, but he adjusted beautifully and played on top of the piled up books and records and furniture.

Only one thing occurred which had not happened before. When the alarm clock rang, it gave him a terrible fright. As the alarm woke me, I heard him jump off his sleeping-perch, flutter and fly to the edge of his cage. He had been shocked out of his sleep. I went to him and soothed him. I remember telling a friend about the incident, and saying, "That just goes to prove that alarm clocks are against nature." I never again let Fabulous hear an alarm clock, I simply took a chance on waking up in time to get to work.

Yet he had heard an alarm clock before and had shown no indications of being frightened. I could not help but wonder if he was all right, if he had completely recovered from his cold.

When the paint odors were gone, Fabulous again flew through the apartment, his home, lighting on his favorite perching places, soaring through the rooms, knowing every part of the place as his own. His walkway on top of the shower enclosure, the handle of the kitchen faucet, the top of the record shelves. While I was putting the books back on the shelves, he was on my head or on my shoulders singing, chirping, talking. And he sang with the roar of the vacuum cleaner.

"Oh, so pretty pretty. Whatcha doing, baby? Say, huh? Beauty, beautiful."

All was well. Surely there was no need to worry. Things were in order again. We were living our everyday lives. Health and happiness seemed to be ours.

CHAPTER FIFTEEN

IS IT SERIOUS?

Then one Monday morning—it was July 22—I was having my usual cup of coffee in bed, and as was his custom, Fabulous flew over to me and perched on my finger, as bright and chirpy as any bird could be. Then suddenly his right leg gave way, his eyes became glazed; he would have fallen except that his body rested against my thumb. This lasted less than a minute, only a few seconds. I was dumbfounded, I had never seen the like before. "What's the matter, Fabulous? Are you all right?" As I spoke I saw him straighten up, I felt the firm grip of his two feet on my finger. He chirped.

"Of course you are all right," I said. "But what in the world happened?" Now he was acting as if nothing at all had happened—he was looking at me, and chirping and kissing my finger. Maybe he merely lost his footing for a few seconds, I said to myself. I kept a close eye on him while I was getting ready to go to work. There was no lagging of interest as he watched me shave, and he was just as alert as ever as he hopped from one part of me to another while I put on my clothes.

That evening when I came in from work and the following day, Fabulous revealed no signs of illness. Holding him in front of the bathroom mirror, I watched him excitedly kiss his reflection. There was no glazed expression in his eyes which seemed bright and clear again.

But Wednesday morning, about seven-thirty, that strange thing happened again. He was perched on his vanity mirror feeding-perch, happily eating his breakfast, when I saw his right side give way. Again he would have fallen, but I quickly reached out my finger to him and under him, my thumb bolstering him. I drew him close to me, his feet were merely on my finger, not gripping my finger, and I looked into his eyes. They were glazed. A sad expression had come over those black diamond eyes that usually glittered like jewels.

I was stunned. I could not think, I did not know what to think. I took him into the living room, and sitting in the chair next to his playhouse, I kissed him lightly on his right wing shoulder, and softly gave him our singing-whistle, the sound he had taught me, a sound he loved.

For about ten minutes he was silent. Then he began to come out of his daze and uttered a barely perceptible chirp, which seemed to say, "I don't understand what happened." Neither of us understood. In another five minutes he seemed to be back to normal, although not quite so lively. I observed him for a while before leaving for work. If I was late, it did not matter, Fabulous was more important. He flew up to the door-porch of his cage, went inside and began eating. He hopped over to his water cup, took a drink, then hopped back to his feeding cup.

It was certainly strange. Neither time did he appear to be in pain; he was more shocked than pained. But now he seemed to be all right again. That evening and Thursday he was a little quieter than usual, but still there was: *"Talking, singing, playing is Fabulous."* His appetite was the same, a good healthy appetite. I slightly dis-

couraged him from playing because I was afraid
he might exert himself. Those two evenings,
Wednesday and Thursday, he spent most of his
time on my finger while we talked to each other
—he would speak a phrase and I would repeat
after him; he would speak another phrase and I
would again repeat after him; we gave to each
other, back and forth, the singing-whistle.

Surely he is all right, I said to myself, I can't
believe it is anything serious.

But Friday morning I knew it must be serious. It happened again. This time in flight. He
had started to fly from one corner of the
shower enclosure to the other corner. He fell
in mid-flight. I held my breath, quickly opened
the shower door, and leaned down to him.
There was no water in the tub. Fabulous was
there with his wings spread out, and he was
looking up and around for me to help him. I
felt my heart floating in tears. I reached down
and slid my hand under him and lifted him
up. In my hand, he brought himself up onto
my finger as I placed it under him, and leaned
against my thumb. But he had maneuvered
himself with only his left side, his right side
was not working. Again this dazed state lasted
for about ten or fifteen minutes.

I realized I must get him to a doctor. I
wished I had taken him to a doctor the first or
second time it had happened. But it had been
so brief, and he had brought himself out of it,
nature had brought him out of it, whatever it
was, and he seemed to be all right. This time,

the third time, he brought himself out of it again, but he was not as lively as he had been.

Friday morning I called Dr. F., the doctor I had taken him to during his first year, and told him what had happened. He said the bird might have had convulsions and that it could be serious and I should bring him in as soon as possible. Dr. F. had an office uptown in Manhattan and another office in the Bronx. That would be a long trip for a bird in a serious condition.

Someone had highly recommended a doctor in the East Sixties in Manhattan, which, by cab, would not be very far. So I made an appointment with him for Saturday morning, the earliest he could see me.

Friday evening, and Saturday morning while I was getting dressed to take him to the doctor, Fabulous was obviously weak, but he was sitting up, doing a bit of flying, and talking and singing, but not much playing. He looked healthy, but he was not acting healthy.

When we arrived at the doctor's office, he had so many patients waiting, most of them dogs, we had to wait four hours before seeing the doctor. Fabulous was tired and disconcerted about being kept in his cage. His eyes looked weak, they were not sparkling. Most of the time he was quiet, too quiet, but when he did chirp, the chirp seemed to say, "Take me home." His eyes, looking up at me, seemed to say, "Take me home."

Finally, our turn came, Fabulous and I were called into the doctor's office. I told the doctor the symptoms and I told him about the bad cold

Fabulous had in the spring. While I was talking with the doctor, Fabulous hopped over to his feeding cup and had a few bites to eat. The doctor did not rush his examination. He was obviously conscientious, and devoted about thirty minutes in his observation of Fabulous. Still he could arrive at no definite diagnosis.

I received the same impression from him as I had received from the other doctors to whom I had taken Fabulous earlier in his life—that it is sometimes extremely difficult to diagnose and treat a bird's illness, they are so small and so very delicate. This is understandable when you consider how it is often difficult to diagnose and treat even a human being's illness. The doctor said that Fabulous was obviously a sick bird, that it may or may not be a serious illness. His feathers were not puffed and his appetite was still reasonably good. "Possibly the bird has a virus infection as a result of his recent bad cold. However, it could be heart failure or strokes."

I must have turned pale when the doctor said "heart failure or strokes." I felt my own heart sinking and my throat clogging up.

Then the doctor tried to reassure me by saying again. "It may not be serious. We'll have to wait and see." He gave me a tonic for Fabulous and a prescription for aureomycin for him. He told me if the bird collapsed again to hold smelling salts to his cere or try to get him to take a drop of brandy.

I had to have faith. I had to believe Fabulous would be all right. So I left the doctor's office feeling better. Someone in the waiting room, with whom I had been talking before seeing the doctor, looked at me with a question in her eyes, and I answered, "The doctor says it may not be serious."

No, I said to myself, it can't be heart failure or strokes. It is some kind of virus infection. The doctor said it could be that. The tonic and the aureomycin will get him well. It must!

When we arrived home, Fabulous was anxious to get out of his cage. How that bird loved our home! I opened his cage door and he flew out. He started out in a beautiful flight, but fell in the foyer, landing on a bookshelf. I was only a few steps away; I went to him immediately and slid my palm under him. He gave me such a heart-rending, pathetic look, such as I had seen during those flightless months of his first year of life; his eyes pleading, saying: "Why is this happening? Help me. I am a bird. I am supposed to fly." I choked up. I kissed him and I comforted him and told him he would be all right.

Within a few minutes he came out of it and perched upright on my finger, but he was obviously weak. I took him into the living room and sat him on the door-porch of his cage. Then I gave him the prescribed number of drops of tonic in his drinking water. He immediately took a drink and seemed to like it. I closed the living room door and went to the corner drug store to have the prescription filled. The druggist did not have such a small dosage as prescribed by the doctor. He had to send out for it, so he told me to come back in an hour.

I returned home and took a look at Fabulous. He was eating.

I telephoned the doctor and told him that Fabulous had fallen in mid-flight. The doctor tried to reassure me, telling me the medicine would have to have time to take effect. I had told the doctor that Fabulous was not a cage bird but an apartment bird. The doctor said I might let him out for a few hours each day but keep him in his cage most of the time until he was well again.

So I reluctantly closed the door of Fabulous' cage. It was like putting a child to bed who does not want to go to bed. He came over to the near-side of his cage, the side nearest to me, and put his foot on the wires of the cage, clearly inform-ing me he wanted out. I tried to explain to him.

When the hour had passed, I returned to the drug store and picked up the aureomycin and a bottle of smelling salts. I came back and dissolved the tiny tablet in his drinking water and tonic. He went to it and looked at it. The tablet and the tonic together had turned the water dark, almost black. He turned away from it. I was terribly afraid he would not take it, but later in the after-noon, he took a big, long drink.

I kept him in his cage until dinner time. I was not hungry, so I had a light dinner of scrambled eggs. Fabulous loved scrambled eggs and he had his share that evening.

After dinner he took a flight into the bathroom,

then back into the living room. I was happy about that flight. He was perking up. When he went into his cage for a drink, I closed the door again, trying to do as the doctor recommended. I kept him in his cage until nine o'clock, that is when I usually watch an old movie on television, and when he would perch on my finger while we bill-and-cooed. He talked and he sang. Yes, he was certainly feeling better than he had felt in the morning or the day before.

I added my prayers to the tonic and aureomycin.

Sunday was another good day for him, he seemed to perk up a little more. I kept him in his cage most of the day, letting him out while I was shaving, then again at lunchtime and dinnertime, then again at nine o'clock. Each time he was let out he took a few flights. I did not want those precious wings to weaken as they had weakened during his first illness.

Yes, dear God, he recovered from his illness that time, let him recover again, let him live a long, healthy life.

But Monday was a bad day for him. He was not perky. His voice did not ring out. His eyes were not sparkling. He perched quietly in his cage or on his playhouse, now and then weakly giving his bell a ring. Perched on my finger, his beak between my lips, his body hovered as close as possible to my chin, seeking comfort. I gave him our singing-whistle.

He did not have his usual hearty appetite Mon-

day or Tuesday. Tuesday morning I did not see
him drink any of his medicated water. When I
came in from work I examined his cup. If he had
taken a drink it was too little to perceive. I took
the cup in my hand and held it to his beak. He
turned his head away and muttered a pathetic
chirp. I knew he wanted a drink of clear water.
I urged him again to take a drink of the medicated
water but he refused. I washed out his drinking
cup and filled it with clear water and gave it to
him. He drank thirstily. Then he bobbed his head
up and down and uttered a pleased chirp.

Wednesday morning I put the tonic and aureomycin in his water again. Then he drank the
medicated water without protest. That evening
when I came in from work he seemed to be one
hundred percent better. When I let him out of his
cage, he flew onto the top of my head, took two
or three strong, high and healthy flights around
the living room and came back to me. During the
day he had eaten well; that hearty appetite had
returned. It was time for his treat, and he ate the
cracker crumbs from my lips with pleasure and
fun, sometimes playing with the cracker. I
cooked a pork chop for dinner and as he was
pecking the meat from the bone, he again re-
minded me of a dog gnawing a bone. He was
feeling better, much better, so of course I felt
better.

If a stranger had seen him, so proud and lively,
the stranger would not have thought Fabulous
had ever been sick a day in his life. Fabulous was
feeling so good, loving life so much, revealing

that tremendous will to live, I knew—how could I doubt it?—I knew he must, he would get well again.

That Wednesday evening after dinner! I shall never forget how beautifully he sang, even more beautifully than that evening nearly five years ago when he had regained his ability to fly. He could not talk then. Now he could talk. Perched on top of his cage, he talked a blue streak; singing his words, he seemed to be trying to go through his entire vocabulary, over and over again. The words I remember most clearly are words I shall never forget:

"Happy, happy bird . . . My name is Fabulous . . . I love you . . ."

Liltingly singing the story of his life.

CHAPTER SIXTEEN

GONE

That lovely evening—how the words streamed out of him!—but it was his Swan Song.

Thursday morning he was listless, not completely listless; it took more than sickness to cause Fabulous to be completely listless. But obviously he was not feeling well. He talked a little, but so softly I could hardly distinguish his words. When I was ready to go to work I put him in his cage; he gazed at me yearningly as I left. During my lunch hour, I rushed home and took a look at him. He looked a little better; he had eaten, not much, but at least something, and he had taken some of his medicated water. I went back to work, praying to God that Fabulous would soon feel well again.

But Thursday evening he felt the same as he had felt in the morning. That night, before going to bed, for an hour or so, Fabulous rested his beak between my lips and again hovered as close to my chin as he possibly could.

Did he know? Did he have a premonition? Had he known Wednesday while he sang his Swan Song? Did his instinct tell him what was going to happen? Only God knows the mystic answer.

Friday morning, August 2:
As always he watched me while I shaved. When I finished shaving he flew up to the shower enclosure. Was he a little stronger or was I only wistfully thinking? I had thought he seemed a little stronger. But when I went into the bedroom, while I was taking a tie from the tie-rack,

I heard the flutter of wings. Then I heard the
wooden coat hanger knock against the metal coat
hanger which held one of his magnifying mirrors. Those sounds I had heard many times
before—the sound of Fabulous flying, flying to
his coat hanger perch in front of his mirror.

Now I heard a thump. My heart paused, but I
did not pause. I knew what had happened: Fabulous had fallen in flight again. I rushed to him and
opened the shower door. He had fallen on the
window-sill. His wings were spread with a slight
flutter and he was looking back at me, his eyes
asking for help. I slid my hand under him and I
tried to help him perch upon my finger. He
couldn't. He was struggling. His wings, still
spread, were fluttering; his head lifted up, then
fell, then lifted with open beak. There was no
sound of gasping, but he was obviously gasping,
struggling for life.

With my beloved bird in the palm of my hand,
I rushed into the kitchen where I had placed the
bottle of smelling salts next to the brandy on the
work-table. As I reached for the bottle of smelling salts with my right hand, my left hand was
near the top of the work-table; Fabulous, in his
struggle for life, slid from my hand onto the
work-table, just his body—his head was leaning
on my forefinger, his finger-perch. Then so
quickly it happened, before I could open the bottle, his head lifted, his beak opened for life; I
heard a squeak, softer than the squeak of a mouse,
and his head fell against my forefinger.

I realized what had happened the instant, the

split-second, it happened, but I could not believe it. I called him: "Fabulous!" The bottle was opened and I drew him into my palm, calling him and holding the smelling salts to his beak. Calling in a cry: "Fabulous! Don't leave me, Fabulous! Fabulous!" There was no response. His eyes had closed, the sparkle had gone away. But I could not believe he was gone. I knew, but I could not believe. With one hand I opened the bottle of brandy, poured some into a cup, and placed his beak to the cup. He did not drink. My fingers opened his beak and I let a drop of brandy fall onto his tongue. The drop of brandy rolled off. Breathing into his beak, trying to blow the breath of my life into him, I went into the living room. I rang the bell at the top of his ladder. He had always responded to that bell. Now he did not respond.

My beloved Fabulous.

I became hysterical and I collapsed on the floor, my entire body trembling as the tears poured out of me—except my left hand where he lay in my open palm. It was strangely still, as still as his dead body. I was like a child again, weeping; yet I was a man enough to release my grief. Thus the child and the man became one and there was no distinction, and there was no need for any distinction, for there are times when the inner child is wiser than the external man and must guide the man beyond his grief.

After a while I gathered myself together well enough to call my employer and tell him I would not be in to work. He understood and sympathized with me. Not long ago his parakeet had died; it, too, had been a little over five years of age.

I called a friend. I did not need to tell her what had happened. She knew Fabulous had been sick and she knew from the sound of my voice when I cried her name, she knew the end had come. "Oh, no, no. I'm so sorry," she said. She knew what it is to lose a loved one.

I did not know what to do. I felt utterly lost. I had lost my love, my loving Fabulous. But how could it be true? He was still so beautiful, still in the palm of my hand. His beautiful feathers were as soft as a living dream.

I called Dr. F. and told him what had happened and asked him what I should do and asked him if there was anything he could do.

"There is nothing that can be done." the doctor said. "The bird is obviously deceased. From what you tell me, it seems he died of a stroke. A blood clot. Blood trying to pass through the vessels of the brain sometimes becomes clotted; if it manages to pass through as it apparently did the first four times he collapsed, the patient lives; if the blood clot does not pass through the vessel, the patient dies or becomes wholly or partially paralyzed."

Technically Fabulous was dead.

My heart could not accept his death. I was weak with grief. I went to bed with Fabulous in my palm. I did not stay in bed long. I went into the living room and brought the large Rembrandt Bible back to bed with me. I loved Fabulous so much I could not bear his death alone. I had to have God's word help me. I read various passages in the Bible and as I was reading, his feet and his body grew stiff in my hand.

I carressed him, for a long time I carressed him. The stiffness went away, his body became soft again. In my state of mind, dazed and dimmed by his death, I thought I had massaged life back into him. I thought a miracle was happening. While caressing him I had been praying that a miracle would happen and I had been reading in the Bible about miracles.

I still had to believe, believe, have faith, faith, never give up.

The morning was gone. I knew that Dr. F. was in his office in the East Bronx in the afternoon. I placed Fabulous on a handkerchief in his playhouse cage, and took him in a taxi to the doctor's office. In the taxi I could not keep my hand away from him. I continued to pray. Prayers can be of help at anytime, and in a time of tragedy they can be a source of strength.

When we arrived at the doctor's office, the nurse who was Dr. F.'s assistant, came into the waiting room. She took one look at Fabulous, and said, "He's gone, sir."

"Isn't there anything can be done?" I asked. "Are you sure?"

"Yes, I'm sure. There's absolutely no sign of life left in him. You see he isn't breathing, his heart has stopped."

"Yes, I know, but . . ."

"It's hard to believe, I know . . . I understand.

It's hard to give him up. Look, when I pass my finger over his eyes there is no reflex, no response. Would you like me to dispose of his remains for you?"

"No. Thank you anyway. I think I should do that."

"Would you like me to call a cab for you?"

"No. I'll go by subway. Could you tell me how to get to the nearest subway station."

She directed me to a bus that would take me to the subway station which was quite some distance away. She made no charge for officially pronouncing Fabulous dead.

Yes, I had to accept his death. I had known the instant it happened. Now I had to believe even in death as I had believed in his life. I had to face it and live over and beyond the grief that comes with death.

Before I had left for the East Bronx, I had called my friend who lives near Ft. Tryon Park and arranged to spend the evening with her. Tragedy needs the company of friends.

She would not be home from work until six-thirty. So I went to the Park to wait. Walking toward the Park, I passed an abandoned subway entrance, old and locked; the sides are made of iron grill work. Beneath the overhanging roof and behind the grill work there were a number of bird's nests.

I heard the chirping of birds. I looked up and in plain view I saw a mother sparrow feeding two baby sparrows—their beaks were wide open, chirping and very much alive. The mother sparrow looked down at me, she did not fly away, but she kept an eye on me while attending to her baby birds.

Nature was telling me that life goes on, nature replenishes itself. They were a comfort to me.

I walked deep into the Park and sat down on a bench, overlooking the Hudson River. I took Fabulous out of the playhouse-cage, opened my shirt, and placed him inside my shirt, next to my heart.

A squirrel ran up and down a tree. Birds flew about, darting from one tree to another. Two or three birds hopped along a rock embankment and found some water that had been caught in a crevice during a recent rainfall. Now the sun was shining brightly. A slight breeze rustled the living leaves of the living trees. My heart was aching, but nature was alive. I had to see it living; believe in the living, even in the face of death, especially in the face of death, believe in the living. A beetle crawled across the back of the bench. I watched him. I was pleased to see him. He was alive. Moving. Living.

When it was time for my friend to be at home, I left Fort Tryon and went to her apartment. We embraced and I wept again. I had to let the grief flow out with tears. Such a little bird, such a big love! During the evening, I talked a great deal about Fabulous, talking out as much of the grief as I could release.

She helped me plan to put him away. I did not want to put him away the first night of his death.

I needed to keep his remains with me one more night and day. We arranged to have dinner the following night, Saturday, then we would go into the Park and find a place for Fabulous.

That night at home alone with the dead Fabulous—without the talking, singing, chirping Fabulous—I felt as if a rake had scraped across my chest and belly. All the tears and all the talking had not taken away all the grief and all the pain. I wept again at the departure of that tremendous little feathered lover.

Going to bed I again placed him on the open Bible next to me in bed. I slept with the spirit of his love. Perhaps this would have been morbid, except somehow, I don't know just how, but somehow, the open Bible kept it from feeling morbid. I had to face it all.

Saturday evening, near Fort Tryon Park, there with my friend I talked and talked about Fabulous, not even trying to control my feelings, letting them pour without restraint. It was not a time for control. The channels of grief must be opened till all the deep painful grief has streamed out. Then a memory of sadness may come and go, but the memory and the heart live, unharnessed, not held back, not held down by the hard stones of solidified, unshed tears.

Now it was time to put away the remains of my darling Fabulous. I put his favorite bell-mirror in the bottom of his bathhouse; I wrapped him in a handkerchief and placed him on the mirror. My body trembled. I wrapped the bathhouse in aluminum foil and sealed it with scotch tape. It became a shining tomb.

Shortly before ten (the closing time of the Park) my friend and I went into the Park. We found a secluded spot, one where picnickers were not apt to go, on a steep and wooded hillside. I had brought along a paint scraper to use in digging his grave, but that night I decided not to put him underground. He was a bird. We chose a tree and I marked the tree with the paint scraper. I placed him on the ground, close to the tree. I had brought along his bell-ladder, his first toy, the bell he loved so much. I stood it upright between the tree and his shining tomb. The bell-ladder became a bell-cross. My friend helped me gather foliage and we covered his shining tomb. We placed stones over and around the foliage in a somewhat natural way.

Few have lived long without knowing the stark tragedy of death and the deep feeling of emptiness left behind after a beloved has departed.

I loved Fabulous as much as any human being I have ever loved. My love for Fabulous and his love for me was the sweetest and most beautiful love I have ever known.

Coming home that night, I paused at my door. There would be no chirp to greet me. The apartment was terribly empty, dreadfully alone.

Fabulous was gone.

CHAPTER SEVENTEEN

A YOUNG PRINCE & SOMETHING MIRACULOUS

The living must go on living, not merely dragging on. Respect for the dead, respect for the life the dead one lived, must be revealed through flowing tears. Yet tears are not enough. Continued activity must go along with the flowing release.

Life must always outlive death. A mother sparrow and the chirping of two baby sparrows clearly, even in the dimness of my sorrow, revealed that to me the very same day Fabulous died.

One life had gone out of the world; two came in.

Sunday evening, friends living near me on Long Island, invited me to dinner. When I came home Sunday night, I paused again at my door, even longer than the night before. I could hardly bring myself to open my door and go into my songless apartment. For more than five years a beautiful winged life had given me the company of love.

I knew I had to do something about it. I had told myself during his first illness that if he did not live, I would go out as soon as possible, on the third day if I could, and buy another parakeet. Sunday the pet shops were closed. Monday, immediately after work, I went to a pet shop in Manhattan. As it happened, they had received a new shipment of baby parakeets that afternoon, just a few hours before I arrived. The new ones were in two long lines—a double-shelf—of small cages, one or two birds per cage. I walked up and

down in front of the long, colorful lines of birds.
They were all from four to six weeks of age. I
lingered, not wanting to rush myself, trying to
make up my mind.

One little rascal was making quite a hubbub
with his chirps, and hopping and fluttering about
from one part of his cage to another. He was
ignoring the other parakeet in the cage with him.
I saw him crawling around the wires of the cage;
he wanted out of there. I placed my finger between the wires of his cage. He did not flutter
away from my finger. He was not afraid. Without
biting me, he simply took a little skin of my finger
between his beak and looked up at me. His eyes
were shining, sparkling, dancing with life. Life!

He helped me make my choice.

He was the one.

I did not let the salesman put him in a small
cardboard box. That had frightened Fabulous.
Having discarded Fabulous' cage and playhouse
(in case there had been any virus infectious
germs), I bought a new cage for the new bird. I
had the salesman spray the cage. Then he put the
new bird inside. The bird immediately hopped
upon the center swing perch. I bought new supplies and new toys. The salesman put them inside
the cage and wrapped it, leaving an opening at
the top around the handle of the cage. The bird
looked around and up, his eyes examining everything that was happening.

In the taxi, I looked down at him; through the
opening he looked up at me, and chirped in wonder. His eyes and his chirps might have been

saying: "What a busy day. This morning I was shipped from somewhere to the pet shop. Now I am being moved somewhere else. I won't let it bother me. I'll simply swing." The movement of the taxi caused the swing to move back and forth.

Home.

I was not alone.

That evening I gave him a name. I called him Prince, and I said to him: "Fabulous was the King of birds. Now you are a beautiful young Prince, a blue Prince, who has come along to take the place of the King who had to go away."

Something very strange, something almost miraculous happened.

In early September, I went to Fort Tryon Park to visit the burial place of Fabulous. I went directly to the place in the Park and to the tree where I thought I had placed his tomb on the ground. It was not there. I had marked his tree but there was no marking on this one. I looked around and a few feet away I saw the glitter of foil, the foil in which I had wrapped his bathhouse.

During the month of August there had been two very heavy rainstorms. The tree under which I had placed Fabulous had fallen down over him. I walked over to it, the plastic bathhouse was not crushed. The ladder with the bell on top, the bell-cross, was still in an upright position.

God-Nature blew the tree down over him to cover him and protect his remains. The tree

could not stand up to his death. The tree might
have been me—although I had fallen to the floor,
trembled and wept the rains of tears, I was not
broken—instead, God broke the tree near the
roots and shielded that adorable creature. Of all
the trees around, his was the only one within
sight which had fallen down. I pulled some of the
bark from the tree—large pieces had fallen loose
with the falling of the tree—and covered the
glimmering foil.

I walked away, feeling that nature is taking
care.

A month later I went into the Park again. On
my way to his burial place, I stopped half-way
there and picked a flower to place on his tomb. I
do not know the name of the flower, it was a
flower that was not in bloom at the time of his
death; the stem was long and green, the petals
were white, and the center was yellow-orange.
When I came to the fallen tree, the very same
type of flower was growing from beneath the
fallen trunk and over his tomb, peering out at me
with its yellow-orange eye-center. As I was walking toward the tree, I saw only the one flower;
when I came close to the tree, looking on the
other side of it, I saw a cluster of these flowers
growing there, huddled against the tomb of
Fabulous. It had not been necessary for me to
pick the flower I had in my hand, nature had
taken care of the matter. I placed the picked
flower by the growing flowers. I gazed around
and there were no other flowers within sight.

I walked away feeling that this is hard to believe, feeling again that something almost miraculous had happened.

Yet nature is miraculous.

Now at this moment, and throughout most of the time while I have been writing the life and death of Fabulous, the new bird, the young blue Prince is on my shoulder.

He is beginning to talk:

"Pretty pretty baby."

"Pretty pretty bird."